How In Hell Can I Change?

Wayne Sutton

© Copyright 2009

Edited by Shae Cooke and Betsy Gordon

Formatted by Sunny Kapoor **(www.publishinggurus.com)**

Copyright © 2009 by Wayne Sutton

All rights reserved. No part of this book may be reproduced or transmitted in any form or by any means, electronic or mechanical, including photocopying, recording, or by any information storage or retrieval system, without written permission from the author, except for the inclusion of brief quotations for a review.

Endorsements

"Wayne Sutton truly has the gift for writing. Combine that with his understanding of the life changing grace of God, and you have a very understandable and powerful book. For those who have tried and failed to gain dominion over certain aspects of their life, this is good news! The yoke is easy and the burden is light. You will find in this book the overlooked truth that the adversary fears the most, and you will rejoice at a whole new way of seeing things. I have preached the fullness of God, and our completeness in Him for years; and I heartily recommend "How in Hell Can I Change" as a cutting edge message for this generation."

Rick Manis – author of Fullness and Heaven on Earth University www.RickManis.com

"Wayne Sutton has a passion to see people walk in truth and righteousness. This book has what it takes to awaken the minds of God's people to experience that truth to set them free from religious traditions of men. I highly recommend this book to everyone desiring to know Christ in a new and fresh way."

Dr. Jeremy Lopez, www.identitynetwork.net

"A crazy title, yet interesting story! A must have for all Christians! Wayne Sutton is a powerful man of God who understands the things of God on a profound level. His new book is a must have in this season of your life. Ask God & buy today! You will be glad you did. Also check out some of his other literature, he knows how to make people think "CHANGE"."

Stephen Choate, www.speakgodspeak.com

"Wayne Sutton in his book How In Hell Can I Change takes you on a journey that clearly lays out biblical principles of how to live a life of victory. Overcoming the daily obstacles and hurdles that we face. The biggest obstacle, you will find out in this book, that we will ever face is SELF. It is all about renewing our thought process through the Word of God and acting upon what we read. Wayne teaches us how to do this in this book. How In Hell Can I Change will discipline, transform, and unlock your mind as you read it.

As a pastor, I would recommend this book for every Pastor to have in his/her library. It is one that would greatly benefit your staff and leaders as well. After the reading of How in Hell Can I Change, it has caused a change in my thought process of how I view myself and how I view others. I know that this book will change your perspective as well and encourage you in your journey to live a life of victory!"

Diane Nutt – President and Founder of Dove Ministries , www.dove-ministries.com

"If the title of this book catches your attention, then buy this book now! If the title offends you however, then buy several copies… one for yourself, and one for everyone who has ever influenced your religious beliefs!"

Rome Batchelor, www.ControversialChristianity.com

Dedication

I dedicate this writing to one and one alone, to my Lord and savior Jesus Christ. The day will come when I will lay my crown down at your precious feet, yet today I begin with this manuscript. I dedicate this book to you, my Lord, for you are everything to me. I am gracious for your love and your sacrifice, and every day I receive that mysterious and wonderful transformation by your spirit – from glory to glory. Jesus, I dedicate this book to you, a small way of saying, I love you.

Acknowledgments

I want to thank everyone who has influenced my life, especially those who led me to the truth of Jesus Christ. To my son Kelton, and the rest of my family and friends, thank you, for your influence has molded my beliefs and forged within me a burning desire to see people truly changed by God's spirit and his love.

To my beautiful wife Candace I must extend a special word of gratitude. Your support in our ministry is only surpassed by your true heart of love and compassion, both towards God and towards others. You are truly a gift in my life, and in so many ways an example for me to follow.

To my pastors and spiritual leaders, both current and in the past, I owe you for your dedication and for believing in me, even when I didn't believe in myself.

Also, a special thank-you to Shae Cooke, for taking my thoughts and my heart, expressed through my writing, and for making them actually available in print. This book would not be what it is without your gracious assistance.

Table of Contents

Introduction — 9

Part One: *Stop Struggling*

Chapter One: Change, Not Resistance — 13
Chapter Two: For Goodness' Sake — 21
Chapter Three: How The Hell Can I Do This? — 31
Chapter Four: Starve the Dog — 37
Chapter Five: The Truth and Nothing But For Transformation — 51
Chapter Six: Have I Got A Deal for You! — 63
Chapter Seven: Transparency for Transformation — 71
Chapter Eight: Reprogram Your Consciousness — 83
Chapter Nine: Faith in the Positive Power — 91
Chapter Ten: Cross Works vs. Cross Walks — 99

Part Two: *The 5 R's for Transformation*

Chapter Eleven: *Repent* & Change Your Life For *Ever!* — 111
Chapter Twelve: *Release* the Works — 121
Chapter Thirteen: Become a Wide *Receiver* — 129
Chapter Fourteen: *Remind* Yourself, GOD IS GOOD — 143
Chapter Fifteen: *Rest* in Jesus — 155
Chapter Sixteen: *A Lifetime of Life Changing* — 167

About the Author — 175

*A page for your own notes is included at the end of each chapter. You may wish to use this to comment on the chapter, or to add verses of Scripture that speak to you personally.

Introduction

Most people see things in the world they would like to change, or have problems or challenges in their own lives that they would like to see transformed. Changing the bad to good, the wrong to right, and the evil to pure is a hope we can all share in. So how do we find the change that we are searching for? And is the fact that we are Christians truly enough? Is our salvation a promise of peace and overcoming power, or is our salvation instead a guarantee for despair, trouble, and persecution?

We can have change in our life and in the Church! God promises transformation, and it is a *true* transformation from the Spirit of God Himself.

However, there is a serious lack of understanding and revelation about who we are in Christ Jesus and what Christ truly has accomplished. Because of that lack of revelation, Christians continue to struggle: we cry out, and we search for the answers to the seemingly endless problems in our lives. We search the Church, we search the world, we search others, and we even adhere to the lies from the pits of hell – looking for a solution to help us overcome a lifetime of sin, addictions, guilt, condemnation, or shame... *only to realize that we have not truly found the answers.*

Even as Christians, we tend to look everywhere but the proper place, and that causes us to cry out "How in the world, how in the Church, how in HELL can I change?"

I have titled this book "How in HELL?" because without even knowing it, most people look directly into the lies and deception from the very pits of HELL in futile attempts to fix their broken lives, and the lives of others.

If you have struggled with your Christian life and cannot seem to change from old ways; if you are living with the shame of secret sin; or if you feel guilty that you just cannot stop something in your life that keeps you from going to that next level in Christ Jesus, this book will help you, or someone you love.

You will need your Bible, a mind open to the truth, and perhaps a notebook. Get ready for a little paradigm shifting and some pleasant (and not so pleasant) surprises as we expose the lies that cause you to say, "I've tried, I can't, it's futile." It may hurt a little – but the result is truth, and true transformation by the Spirit.

Wayne Sutton

*"It's the small decisions, the everyday choices that seem so irrelevant at the time, that form not only our lifestyle – but actually create our destiny.
Choose your actions wisely."*

– Wayne Sutton

Chapter One
Change, Not Resistance

It is amazing and sometimes frightening how our entire life can seem to shift for the worse in an instant. However, usually the suddenness of our predicament is the product of an insidious process of erosion. It wears away our joy and happiness, and ultimately weakens our soul until *voilà* – that eye-opening moment when it is too late.

One particularly brisk Thursday morning would be Snyder's eye-opening moment. "You're under arrest, place your hands behind your back!" bellowed the high-school campus undercover police officer, as he slapped the cold handcuffs around the young man's wrists.

The bag of marijuana that the seventeen-year-old had, only seconds before, purchased from a student dropped to the floor. The officer caught them right in the switch of the crumpled twenty-dollar bill, stolen from his mother's purse that morning, for the small plastic bag of dope.

Snyder paled, hung his head, and stared at the bag where it had fallen as the officer explained the charge. As quickly as the bag had fallen, so did his hope and dreams—with a horrible thud.

How could I let this happen? The morning bell rang for school; but he would not be heading to class anytime soon, he was sure of it. *What next?* He shuddered at the thought of the darkness that lay ahead. It wasn't so much the idea of being behind bars…but *His parents – how could he face them?*

The teenager had only seen his father's face flush with anger and disappointment a few times in his life. It was not characteristic of Dad's usually friendly, kind, and patient demeanor. Snyder always avoided upsetting him; how would Dad react now? And what of his mom? How could he muster the strength to see her? It would mean looking into her soft green eyes, flowing with tears because of his bad choices.

He feared seeing their hurt more than he feared prison. They had always had a close relationship built on trust. As the officer led him away, Snyder was not sure he would get to wherever he was going without crumbling.

***

Snyder was a typical teenager in almost every way. He "endured" his daily classes in anticipation of the final school bell, which meant time with his buddies shooting hoops or playing video games. More of a follower than a leader, however, Snyder struggled with his self-esteem. Equating popularity with the antidote to his happiness, he played along with many of their escapades. Sometimes he vied for the attention of his peers with antics of his own, playing pranks, or joking around, becoming a class clown of sorts.

Indeed, he found a niche of acceptance, albeit an unhealthy one; because his growing dependence on the approval of his peers did not sate his real, deep-seated needs. It would prove his demise, especially as his friends cruised into increasingly dangerous waters.

"Snyder, you gotta try this," his friend Brad said one Saturday night, handing him a joint. Curious, because he had heard the stuff made you feel good, and not wanting to look un-cool, Snyder took the bait. "Sure, why not?"

Just as his cravings for acceptance increased his dependence on friends for his happiness buzz, so too did his yen for the synthetic high of the initial toke serve to increase his dependence on drugs. The lethal combination of peer acceptance and pressure, and the yearning for sustained happiness steered him into an increasingly dark pit.

The following weekend, he went deer hunting with some of his friends. They had a "bag" on them, and of course, lots of booze. On a Friday afternoon, behind the mall, a friend gave him a quick toke. Before he knew it, Saturday night's joint became Thursday's nightmare. How long it took the occasional buzz to become an addiction to Snyder is irrelevant. The sad truth is that the teen's life became one of dependency. Although he knew it was wrong, although he desired to change, he did not know how to change. And, he did not know how even to begin to satiate his hunger for what was really his root yearning – joy and acceptance.

How devastating for anyone to hear those powerful words, "You're under arrest!" It's particularly frightening for a young person. But without consequence, an adolescent or teen has only peers and the world to persuade him or her.

The day of Snyder's arrest was routine for the officer, but was a day drenched in fear for the boy. Whatever punishment the authorities would invoke upon him was nothing, compared to the hidden penalty of seeing shame in his mother's eyes, or hearing mistrust in his father's voice. They'd cry out that he was following in his older brother's footsteps. "Where did we go wrong?" they'd wonder, and cast blame on themselves. He knew his mother had always feared he would be swayed the way of Tyler; and now her worst nightmare was coming true. How could he do this to her – to them? How could he disgrace them like that? He knew what was right – why didn't he learn from Tyler's mistakes? Why didn't he heed his parents' guidance?

He was certain. *I'll never take another drug,* he promised himself. *Whatever it takes, I never want to go through this again, or put my parents through it.* As soon as he finished paying for his crime in community service, he'd be on the highway to change, and he'd never look back.

He would never forget his shame, his fear, the jumble of extreme emotions. Those things scarred him for life; but would this experience be enough to transform Snyder? Would the shock of his arrest deter him from a reckless lifestyle? Did the humiliation of being led out of the school in handcuffs make a real difference? How about his sentence from the judge: was it enough to scare him straight? What about the disappointment in his father's voice, or hearing his mother cry from the depth of her heart when the judge passed sentence? Would his breach of their trust and knowing that he caused them such pain provoke him to a U-turn for the better?

Did *any* aspect of the consequences give him the power he needed to turn away – for his own good, for the sake of his future? Sadly, no. None of those things sustained his well-meaning resolve. It took only a few weeks for the peer pressure, his need for approval, and his desire for momentary pleasures to control him once more, and he grasped again for the drugs.

Only seventeen, and Snyder was a drug addict. All that ensued before may have complicated or interrupted the path he was following; but none of it held the sustaining, transforming power to release Snyder from his real prison.

Fast-forward: it's twenty years and hundreds of drug encounters later. Snyder managed to stay out of trouble and not get caught buying drugs. In fact, he was extra careful, and learned how to manage and curb his drug habit enough that he could finish school and get a job that he really enjoyed. Engaged to his best friend's sister, Susan, his life held an outward appearance of stability and happiness.

It was all a mirage.

He still struggled inwardly with the very same problems he had as a younger man. To his friends, his parents, and his fiancée, he was the image of happiness. He learned how to mask his innermost cravings with outward bravado—a wax smile and plenty of charisma.

Your Notes:

"Truly hypocrisy is very real in the church today; more often than not, however, it's not hypocrisy that we see – it is simply a misunderstanding of theology wrapped up in a giant dose of religious prejudice."

– Wayne Sutton

Chapter Two

For Goodness' Sake

Thanks to his parents, Snyder did have a good foundation for life. He held good morals when it came to respecting others, to treating people fairly. Never would he steal or intentionally hurt someone. A generous giver, too, Snyder was always right there when someone asked for help. His thinking was, being a *"good person"* overrode that other "stuff," like drugs or alcohol. He made it to thirty-seven. Who needed church? *After all, he probably did more good,* according to his reasoning, *than many of those religious hypocrites who faithfully went to church every Sunday ...they were no better than he was.* Snyder believed that he did not need God to be a good person.

How many Snyders do you know? Many in the world today are great moral people: they do much good, but they are as sick inside as Snyder was, full of addictions, unmet needs, and afflictions. In short, they are void of God, never having searched for true relationship with Him. They see the self-righteous and the hypocrites, and are quick to justify themselves in comparison. The mind-set is, *"After all, it is better not to be double-minded,"* and *"I do a lot more good than they do."*

Disturbingly, the Church often *has* been hypocritical. The Snyders are right about that. Nevertheless, that fact does not discount or mask their need for the Lord, or ours. Their goodness is camouflage for their neediness, and double-mindedness is their downfall and ours. It is all to the detriment of the growth of the kingdom, and the magnification of God's goodness to the many lost and searching souls who do not find their transformation.

How quick we are to piously judge: not only them, but also even those in our own sphere of Christendom or congregations. We masquerade under the cover of an empty religion that judges or condemns; we self-exalt, even over one another. How will anyone who comes to us see beyond the smoke and mirrors of religion? In a world that is beyond caring and does not deliver the lasting, sustaining hope that any of us need, their only hope *is* God.

Someone like Snyder, if he walked through the doors of a church and laid his life bare -- all that mess hidden below his fabricated exterior -- what would be his chances of coming through saved, healed, and delivered? Would he hear and experience the true Gospel of Jesus Christ, or would he see and feel condemnation and judgment by the recipients of his trust?

There *are* Christians who look upon sinners with hatred and disgust, not compassion and love. It happens every day in the Church. Survey people, even those in your church, today and ask them, "Has the church ever hurt you?" You'll hear "Yes," too often. Only the compassion of God Himself could have led them to Christ, and healed them of the pain of rejection by those who had what they needed but failed to deliver.

I have seen people step aside to avoid the "scum" and "vagrants." They place their Bibles or coats on the chair beside them to pretend the seat is occupied. Heaven help them if they get "too close" to sin. What about introducing them to Christ Jesus, who can make all things new and wash them white as snow? The visitor may be crimson, but what about telling him or her about the transformation possible through the Savior?

We are all guilty of overlooking real need, of judging and condemning those who need *the power* of Christ's work in them. I was guilty and at times, I still am. "God," I cry daily, "Please change me, mold me, transform me;" and He does, in an ongoing work.

Now, Snyder believed that because he had made it thus far on goodness, for goodness' sake, that he did not need God. He thought those other things that fed his innermost needs did an adequate job of it. He could saunter along in life relatively unscathed; fulfill the basics, as long as he held to his core values, which, of course, were empty without God. The core values he lived by in a sense justified his addictions and his secret lifestyle. However, those innermost needs of his were yet unmet; all he had was salve. Those needs were really wounds that required complete healing for true transformation. Only that transformation would take him from a ho-hum existence to a life truly worth living for.

But how to reach Snyder? Whenever his best friend, Tom, asked him to visit his church, Snyder always had a polite excuse at the ready. He was usually busy Sundays anyhow, either nursing a hangover or engrossed in sports, but he could not tell Tom that. Any excuse would do. Snyder's fiancée Susan, Tom's sister, wasn't a Christian either, and preferred to sleep in on Sundays; so church was out of the question.

Tom did not give up. He wasn't pushy, mind you – just determined and steadfast, always asking casually and not making a big deal out of his friend's obvious hang-up about God and religion. "Lord," Tom prayed the same prayer for twenty years. "Let Snyder see his need for You! Help me to reach him with Your love and saving grace."

The love of football was one thing they both held in common. Snyder found it hard to resist when Tom invited him over to watch an important game. "We're ordering pizza. Bring some snacks and come on by."

Snyder had been a huge fan of the game since childhood, when his father tossed him his first football, and then when his dad was teaching him to catch, pass, and tackle. Those days were long since past. Snyder pulled away from the close relationship he had with the man whom he'd once looked up to so much. His lifestyle strained things between them. He saw and spent less and less time with his parents over the years, his own shame causing him to pull away. He wanted that father/son trust and spark back, but did not know how to repair and bridge the chasm that he himself had created – and continued to create.

Snyder stopped by the grocer for a six-pack of beer on his way to Tom's, and arrived to find quite a few people already there. He popped the beer into the cooler, grabbed a few chips off the table already loaded with snacks, and settled in for the game. The first half was exciting and he was right into it, jeering on penalties, cheering on field goals and touchdowns, and swearing a blue streak on unfair plays. At halftime, he refilled, and noted how many more people had come in. The place was packed and they were still filling the living room.

A middle-aged man squeezed into a chair near him to watch the game. Snyder rolled his eyes: the death of the party just walked in. He laughed to himself; the preacher guy needed a shave, and just where was his fancy suit? Darned if he'd watch his "manners" in front of him! As if to make his point, Snyder looked the scruffy minister straight in the eye and took another swig of beer. The guy didn't flinch. Nor did he even twitch when Snyder let out a few expletives, louder than usual. *Put him in a pair of jeans, ditch the Good Book, and he almost looks normal,* thought Snyder. By the end of the night, Snyder concluded that the man *was* normal – a regular guy. He was so easy to get along with, so easy-going, that Snyder almost did not think twice before offering him a beer or cursing an unfair penalty. Snyder waited for rebuke, or at the least, criticism, correction, or condemnation. It never came; the man sided with him on the unfair call and did not whack down his Bible once in judgment of his excesses.

Snyder waited for a reason to reject the man and his beliefs. He waited for an opportunity to be angry: an accusation, a sign like a certain look of disgust, or perhaps a move to another chair; but instead, the man pressed in, to get to know him.

For the first time in a long time, Snyder could relate to someone other than Tom (who he felt was an exception, not the rule). Here was another believer who would restore to him his hope that there was a genuine God who cared, who could transform and help him change things in his life.

That night marked a decided shift. "Wow, Tom," said Snyder after most of the guests had left. "The guy is cool. I need his kind of religion."

Tom invited him to the Thursday Bible study. "It's really casual. No pressure; we just fellowship and study over a bucket of chicken wings."

"Can I bring my beer?" teased Snyder, pushing the envelope good-naturedly.

As promised, he did attend the get-together. No excuses this time. Though he didn't understand everything, Snyder listened to the friendly exchange of thoughts and ideas going back and forth among the assembled, close-knit group of believers. Their concern for each other's welfare impressed him, as did their genuine laughter and spirit of fun. He grew hungrier to know everything he could about this man "Jesus," and to find relationship with Him. Snyder heard testimonies, saw transparency, and experienced people being real with their emotions, their thoughts, and their needs. He heard them get to the root of problems and then access the Solution to their problems, via prayer to a God who seemed extremely personal.

For the first time in his life, Snyder felt God.

A few more buckets of chicken wings and several chapters of the Bible later, and Snyder was right in there asking questions, seeking answers. And at last, deeply convicted by a gentle tug of the Holy Spirit at his heart, he triumphantly came to Christ.

"Thank you, Jesus," he sobbed. He was suddenly realizing how much He needed the Savior, after examining his own life. Falling to his knees and clutching the Bible Tom had given him, Snyder humbled himself before God. "Thank You!" he cried out, with genuine repentance and thanksgiving in his heart.

As so many young-in-Christ believers do, Snyder set out right away, eager to transform his life, live for God, and change the world.

Your Notes:

"There must be a way to change and transform, because all things are possible, for those in Christ Jesus, for those who love the Lord. If we can do "all things through Christ," then transformation is possible."

– *Wayne Sutton*

Chapter Three

How in Hell Can I Do This?

Even with all his newfound dedication and determination, Snyder had no idea how to live as a Christian, or how to please God or the Church. Should he copy Tom? The preacher guy? Some of his new friends in the Bible study group? The self-righteous zealots in the church down the street? He wanted to do the right thing… but exactly what was the right thing?

He felt a conviction to quit drugs and taper off the drinking. But would sex with his fiancée, whom he had committed to marry, be sin, too? Mentally noting what he had observed some believers not doing, he set to work cleaning house, vowing not to save any "junk" that could jeopardize his new commitment and promise to the Lord. *Wow! This will take some work,* he realized; and indeed, it would, because he did not have a clue how to overcome those challenges that would bring change.

"You should live as a Christian," or "Live a godly lifestyle," means little to one who has not been taught what that looks like. Someone like Snyder, who had only glimpsed acceptable model servants of the Lord, would have no idea what to do next. What if he had never had examples in Tom, or in the preacher man? What if he only ever had the notion that Christianity is about legalistic, self-righteous disciplines? Or worse, what if he thought Christianity was a (perverted) view of libertarianism, with Christians using grace as an excuse to live a life full of sin and perversity?

Snyder desired change -- no doubt about that; but it would not be as immediately forthcoming as he originally thought it would. He so wanted to please God, to transform for Him, that Snyder immediately surrendered his drugs and alcohol dependency to the Lord. "Here it is, God."

He told his fiancée, "No more sex before marriage."

His profanity was an obvious problem, and he vowed he would stop. Then he called the cable company and cancelled the "adult" channels. Commendable!

Was he successful? What do *you* think?

His first night was a struggle. The urge for a drug fix was so great that he felt guilty for even wanting it. The wooden box of dope was under his bed. *Weren't these desires supposed to disappear tonight? I'm born again, a new person. Why don't I feel like a new person? Why am I not delivered from these drugs – from my addiction?* Confused by a combination of effects from withdrawal and the euphoric but confusing newness of his salvation, he reached for the box, resisting all the while, but shooting up, nevertheless. With his fix, his head cleared enough to wonder, *Have I lost my salvation because of this sin? Can God really take this addiction away? Why didn't He stop me?*

Welcome to the confusing and real world of the lost. If you have never experienced an addiction, a broken marriage, or a recurrent problem of life or morality, amen!

You are in the minority, because most Christians need help overcoming issues in life that, for the greater part, the Church handles poorly.

Our hearts cry out along with Snyder's, "How in hell can I change? It's all so *confusing*. They tell me:

- God can take away your addictions... *then why am I still addicted?*
- God can heal you of all your sicknesses... *then why am I still sick?*
- God can heal your broken heart... *then why do I still hurt?*
- God can restore all things... *then why am I still broken?*"

Snyder felt tremendous guilt for using drugs the very same day he received forgiveness. Guilt is a death sentence if it's not properly handled. Was it Snyder's fault that he fell to temptation, or was it because he did not know how to resist it? Could it be he tried to change himself?

Snyder tried to change the same way almost everyone tries to change: by *resisting*. Resist the urges, resist the hormones, resist the emotions, resist the confusion, and resist the addictions. Snyder resisted and resisted perfectly well, until he *could not* resist, and *did not*.

When he could not resist the withdrawals from the heroin, when the soft touch of his fiancée brought back memories of their sexual encounters just a few days before, when the chemical addictions and sexual hormones were too much to resist any longer, Snyder gave in.

Snyder fell.

Not from the love and grace of God, but into the lusts of the flesh. He fell into the flesh. Why? He tried to change himself. He attempted to resist the flesh and walk away from his sins by his own power. The guilt and shame of condemnation enveloped him, as he fell into the "performance trap" set up by the enemy to gauge his salvation and relationship with Christ. The trap was failure-based.

Snyder fell, all right, right into the same lie that most Christians fall into every day. It is the lie from the pits of hell itself, a lie that tells us we are saved based on our performance and how well we adhere to a list of laws that often are not even mentioned in the Word of God. The lie fed Snyder is the very one that has damned too many people into a life of condemnation and even hatred for the Church.

There must be a way to change and transform, because "all things are possible," for those in Christ Jesus, for those who love the Lord. If we can do "all things through Christ," then transformation is possible.

We're all weary, and sick and tired of resisting, then failing, then dealing with shame, guilt, and condemnation because we can't get sustainable breakthrough. "Why can't I resist temptation? Why do I fail?" begs answers.

Your Notes:

"The Law cannot justify an individual before God and never was it intended for that purpose. The Law is a tutor to show us our need for a Savior, the need for a Redeemer who will take the curse upon Himself and save us. The purpose of the Law is to show us our transgression of the Law, and our need for the one Savior who can bring us true change by writing the law upon our heart and not on tablets of stone."

– Wayne Sutton

Chapter Four

Starve the Dog

When I asked a close friend of mine how to overcome a certain area of sin in my life, he told me a metaphorical story. I am sure you may have heard it before, or at least one of the story's many versions.

It begins by telling us that we all have both a good side and a bad side living within us, portrayed as black and white, yin and yang, and good and evil, with both forces existing at the same time. Now don't freak out, I am not going New Age on you. I'm using it to illustrate my point that there exists in all of us, a metaphorical "good dog" and "bad dog" within. Think of Satan as the bad dog. According to this philosophy, the dog a person chooses to feed becomes stronger and stronger. Thus, for instance, when you do what is right and good, you are feeding the good dog; and when you do bad things or think upon evil, you are feeding the bad dog. In that way, you give one or the other strength and power. When our bad thoughts or deeds feed the evil dog, it will strengthen until it kills the good dog within you…and then it kills you!

The basic good/bad philosophy is okay, but the rest attributes too much power to the evil dog (Satan). This philosophy implies that only I (not God) can change my devious ways by glossing over them and doing more good than bad, to push the good stuff out. This is not what the Word of God says! There is another way to say *"Sayonara"* to the junk in our lives.

Once I turned my life over to Christ, I found that many questionable desires, thoughts, and even bad habits fell away almost instantly. I felt different and viewed things differently because of the new spiritual birth within me. This was not something I tried to accomplish, and it was not based on me "feeding" or "starving" the metaphorical dogs within me. It was instant, and it was God who performed the spiritual heart transplant.

At the same time, I must face some struggles as I grow into the person Christ wants me to become. I have to stress this to you: I still have struggles within my own life! This is so important both for you to understand, and for me to speak forth; because for too many years, Christians have pretended that their salvation experience removed all of their former obstacles, trials, and temptations. And for way too many years, actually centuries, we have held our trials and temptations behind a veil within the Church, keeping our imperfections out of the sight of our brothers and sisters in Christ for fear of rejection, gossip, and rebuke. We held, or are still holding, these secrets behind a thick cover of shame and guilt.

*****

"How do you guys deal with sexual temptation?" A young single guy at church asked this truthful and liberating question one Sunday afternoon as he chatted with a group of young Christian men. I say this question was liberating because I had, as many Christian singles have, fought the battle for years without having any courage to ask others for help. To ask for help, however, would have torn down that veil, and exposed me and my temptation to a holier-than-thou and righteous church. How could I ever do that?

****

Thankfully, my friend with the courage to ask was a new Christian, and had not suffered decades of religious training. He could ask such a question without feeling condemnation or shame. He had a concern, and he wanted an answer! Wow! That is truly liberating and rare in the Church today!

Resistant To Change

and Resisting Instead of Changing

So many people are in bondage, shackled in chains of despair. They struggle with the same challenges, over and over, without breakthrough. Why do we witness so little change? What causes us to fail? Let me try to answer that in two parts.

First, as humans we tend to resist change. Even when something could be painful, harmful, or deadly to our life, we still tend to resist change and take the path of least resistance. The path of least resistance is often that of staying within our comfort zone despite the potential consequences.

Second, "I should stop" or "I should start" are of the same holding power as resistance to change is. Snyder was thoroughly convinced that he *should* stop drinking, stop smoking, stop using drugs, stop having pre-marital sex, and stop denying Christ around his fellow co-workers. He was also just as convinced that he *should* start reading his Bible more often; he *should* be more faithful in attending Bible study and worship service; and he *should* start making time to share his faith with those co-workers who are with him at least forty hours every week. "Stop" and "start," however, are enemies of the powerful word "change." People unconsciously are drawn towards consistency. The law of consistency says that once someone has set him or herself into a pattern of behavior, even a detrimental pattern, it is natural for them to remain in that behavioral pattern.

Although Snyder wanted to change, with the hope to please God, many people have no inclination to change for a number of reasons.

- *They have a fear of failure.* They are scared to get started doing anything that resembles change. They know that if they are not successful in the process of change, they will be staring failure in the face. A loss of control, whether real or imaginary, causes the person to feel powerless. It is easier – and in their mind, safer – simply to stay as they are now.

- *They are creatures of habit.* Over 80% of the population will retain their religious background as they reach adulthood. That means that if someone was raised a Baptist, then most likely he or she will remain a Baptist. If someone was raised Catholic, then Catholicism will usually remain his or her religious choice. This 80% rule also applies to those who never receive any Christian influence in their childhood. This 80% will almost never begin a relationship with Christ or attend church services regularly. Raising our children in church is surely of the utmost importance in this day of moral decline.

Our lives usually comprise a myriad of habits and routines that we follow repeatedly every day, habits that all run together to make up our life. Even if the habits are dangerous or not beneficial to us, in most cases we still follow our habitual self all the way to the slaughter. Because change goes against our habitual nature, we resist it. We also frequently see failure, because most of us are skilled in the art of "resisting."

Snyder was simply resisting when he pushed away the drugs and alcohol. He was simply resisting when he pushed away his fiancée's sexual advances. He resisted the urge to tell the latest dirty joke around the water cooler. Snyder simply resisted the urges, and did so with the best of intentions.

The decision to resist temptation is great; that is, until the pressures of the habits and addictions overtake the worn-down soul.

In Narcotics Anonymous, as well as other programs, they teach you to notice when you are depressed, tired, hungry, angry, and so on. These emotions trigger the temptation to return to an addictive behavior. Your resistance muscles weaken and collapse under the load of temptation. When you are tempted and when you cannot resist, take note of the triggers that make you fall susceptible.

A friend of mine, Jerry Batchelor, shared a weight-lifting exercise program with me several years ago that clearly illustrates this example. In this weight resistance training, you simply choose an exercise and use the maximum amount of weight against your muscles. Unlike traditional weightlifting exercises however, you do not move the weight up and down for a full range of motion. You actually only hold the *excessive weight* in a way that fully contracts the muscle, and then you just hold it. The more weight you use, the better, because you are trying to quickly overweight the muscle and deplete your energy supply rapidly.

The results were awesome – because despite your willpower, despite your willingness, despite everything, in a matter of just six to ten seconds, your muscles would simply fail from pure exhaustion. The lesson is really a revelation for us. Given enough consistent pressure, the flesh, which is weak, will fail.

Note that this resistance-based training built muscle and helped build strength. In the same way, resisting the urge to dive back into temptations of the flesh can help you strengthen yourself and assist in overcoming during weaker times of temptation!

Yes, you should resist sin, temptation, and destructive behavior instead of simply giving in to the problem. If Snyder felt tempted to use drugs again, then of course, he should have attempted to resist and not do it. Willfully giving in to temptation will only hinder and slow down the process of change, the very transformation that God performs within us. The problem lies within the guilt and shame that haunts us when we do fail.

God's Word tells us to resist the devil and he will flee (James 4:7). However, we should learn how to change properly, and be transformed during the process so we are no longer fighting every trial and temptation. Instead, the process of turning our temptation has to be given to the Lord Jesus Christ. This is the purpose of this book: there has to be a solution to living an overcoming life.

WHAT DO YOU NEED TO CHANGE?

Everyone needs a change in his or her life, in some area, at some time. This is where so much confusion lies within the Body of Christ today. What should you attempt to change in your life? What areas should you simply be content with as they are? What areas are truly sin? And finally, how do you either change yourself or change the specific areas in your life?

One of the biggest challenges for change is attempting to clearly see and admit our need for the change in any area of our life. Denial of our need to change, or the complete ignorance of our need for change is one reason we must rely on someone other than ourselves to help us. Although we have spiritual leaders who can counsel us and lead us, we will devote our time and attention in this book to the One who will always lead you and transform you without fail… Jesus Christ.

*****

Snyder had been a drug addict ever since his teenage years. The addiction only led to deeper problems within his life as he dove deeper into depression. Shame and guilt fueled his hopelessness. He knew something in his life needed changing.

It is a biblical fact that we all have a sinful nature. The Old Testament Law makes that clear. However, many in the Church misconstrue the Law as being something we must keep to the letter, or else. Where is grace? Where is mercy? People are of the mistaken mind-set that Christianity is a set of do's and don'ts, and as long as we do this and don't do that, we'll score points in heaven, have abundant life, and be saintly and holy. Nonsense! If we try to earn our salvation by keeping the Law of Moses, even a part of it, we step into our own self-justification. In so doing, we actually shun Christ Himself. In our attempts to please God by earning our salvation, we are exercising the spirit of antichrist, proclaiming to Jesus through our futile attempts to overcome, that His sacrifice was not enough. "Here, let me help You, Jesus…" Ouch!

> *Knowing that a man is not justified by the works of the law, but by the faith of Jesus Christ, even we have believed in Jesus Christ, that we might be justified by the faith of Christ, and not by the works of the law: for by the works of the law shall no flesh be justified (Galatians 2:16 NKJV).*

The Law cannot justify an individual before God, and never was it intended for that purpose. The Law is a tutor to show us our need for a Savior, the need for a Redeemer who will take the curse upon Himself and save us. The purpose of the Law is to show us our transgression of the Law, and our need for the one Savior who can bring us true change by writing the law upon our heart and not on tablets of stone.

*****

"Should I also stop smoking cigarettes?" Snyder faced many addictions and questioned many of his lifestyle practices and habits. Did his habits and addictions disqualify him as a Christian? Would the Church accept him while he was in the process of changing and maturing in his faith? Would you accept him in his process of change?

Snyder examined the lives of other Christians when he was looking for a change in his life. His sister had been a Christian for a number of years, and always displayed love and gratitude towards others. Naturally, Snyder gravitated to her, and sought her out when he looked for guidance in his Christian walk. He could not resist her outpouring of love and mercy, particularly as he went through various stages of growth.

The young man's co-worker Giles was another story. Giles was a Christian and a good friend, but relied on his own view of morality to justify his salvation or condemn those he felt did not live up to his personal standard of holiness. Taking Giles's mind-set as an example, Snyder hesitated to spend much time with a Christian friend named Tom, who would have been great for him. Who would want to spend time with someone who constantly judges or condemns? Snyder was afraid Tom would think as Giles did.

"You should not be smoking, that is a sin."
"The Bible says that you should not drink alcohol."
"I can't believe you just used that type of language. D-A-M-N is a curse word!"
"You should pray at least an hour a day. That's what I do."

Wow, talk about a mother lode of guilt, condemnation, and shame! It's a tidy condemning package, all in the name of the Lord.

I'm not making light of sin: sin is serious. However, if you were a babe in Christ and barely walking, what would you want to hear: a set of laws that if you break them will condemn and punish you, or encouragement about God's grace and mercy, His empowerment and strength to overcome, the importance of transparency before God? Truth comes from the truth in Jesus Christ, not in keeping of the Mosaic Law or the law of manmade legalistic religious doctrines.

> *O foolish Galatians! Who has bewitched you that you should not obey the truth, before whose eyes Jesus Christ was clearly portrayed among you as crucified? This only I want to learn from you: Did you receive the Spirit by the works of the law, or by the hearing of faith?* (Galatians 3:1-2, NKJV).

O foolish Galatians, who has bewitched you! Apostle Paul was firm in his rebuke of the doctrinal teachings from the Galatians' church to the believers. Although saved by grace and their faith in the finished work of the cross, they had turned back to the keeping of the Law, in a futile attempt to maintain their salvation. Ridiculous? Totally, and yet common still, even today.

Here lies the main problem in the teaching between grace and law. When we go back to the Law, either the Mosaic Law or legalistic manmade laws of the Church, we fall into the bewitching that the Galatians fell into, that of discrediting the finished work of the cross, and discrediting and making light of Jesus' perfect sacrifice – all for the ability to display our own self-righteousness.

So what then? Should we sin so that grace may abound more? No! Obviously, we should not sin, and likewise we should not teach others to sin. The problem is when we as the Church hold up our standards to measure another, and we have the nerve to determine if their salvation is legitimate or not. As the Galatians behaved, so do we. As the Pharisees behaved, so do we; and as Lucifer himself condemns and persecutes, so do we... God forbid.

The solution?

Transparency. Yep. The ability to be transparent and admit your sins and struggles is a crucial part in overcoming and achieving true change. There may be times you are transparent with others, and times when you should not be. Being transparent, however, has to start with your *openness* with yourself and with God. Even though God is already aware – He knows everything about you, everything you've hidden and buried deep, and those things you may not be aware of -- it is vital to take time with Him. It is critical to lay bare your heart before God, sharing your faults, your weaknesses, and even your thoughts, good or bad. This is a *crucial* step toward building a deeper relationship with the Father.

While in time of open communication, that is, prayer to the Father, you may also discover areas within yourself that need transformation. That takes times of listening, in two-way conversation. I discovered areas that needed transformation for years, but I could not see they were there until the Lord revealed them to me. Hear what He says. Guaranteed, it is the Truth.

Your Notes:

"To change the whole world, to reform a government, and to resurrect a dead nation, is all as simple as sharing the truth of Jesus Christ with the people and expecting Christ to transform them from glory to glory."

– Wayne Sutton

Chapter Five

The Truth and Nothing But For Transformation

Revolts and revolutions have torn at our very souls, as generations have fervently sought to transform the world into the utopia we imagine it could be. Countless governments form and countless governments fall in this endless search. I am persuaded that the rivers of the world could not hold the tears, nor the oceans of the deep contain the blood that has been spilled in our futile search for truth and happiness. We have destroyed lives and crushed hopes for countless centuries, seeking to change people through governing and ruling them. We have looked at law, whether biblical law or man's judicial law, to change the heart of man. We have failed.

The Church itself has committed the same atrocities in its continuous search for holy perfection. Division is clear, as we stare into the differences between Jews and Christians, Buddhists and Atheists, and even differences within the Christian faith! This holds true not only for religious differences outside of Christianity, but even within our own denominational communities. These prejudices have corroded our hearts for generations, leaving our souls covered with scales of pride and self-righteousness.

Who is right and who is wrong? When can we admit our mistakes, and how can we change the mistakes of others? Why can't the Baptists understand the working of the gifts of the Spirit? Why don't the Pentecostals grasp the concept of grace, instead of burdening their people with legalism? Why don't the Catholics understand the principles of the Lutheran reformation? Why so much confusion and pain from the very Church that is supposed to offer faith, hope, and love to a dying world? We ask many questions, and we dig for a multitude of answers. The excavation process in our search for answers is good; but we have to dig in the right places if we ever hope to uncover the ancient truths that the enemy has buried beneath the sands of religion.

Change What?

What needs changing in the world? What needs changing in the Church? It would take volumes to list everything, and I still wouldn't be able to cover all that needs change and transformation. So, too, how could you be certain that some of the things I list are not the product of my own opinion or religious beliefs? There are absolutes, of course, on which the Bible is completely clear, like adultery, murder, and greed -- but what about those grey areas or issues that the Bible doesn't list?

There are so many different denominations of Christianity, and each one seems to have made its own list of what is right and what is wrong! This makes it difficult sometimes for a person to discern what sin *is* in his or her own life, and what it *isn't*. To try to dig, to sift through a host of fabricated rules, is next to impossible, if we are to discern what is right for or what is wrong in our life.

How Do I Identify Sin?

This was Snyder's challenge as he began his walk as a Christian. It is also a challenge for most sincere Christians caught in legalistic religious systems. So, how do we identify sin in our lives, and how do we approach it?

Well, let us start with the latter question. First, we must all admit that we are not yet perfected. As individual Christians, and as a Church body, we are still in the process of maturation. Transformation will not be effective if we ignore the need for it in our lives.

How do you know that you need change in a particular area? If any area of your life does not line up with the Word of God, then it needs to be transformed and realigned by the Spirit of God. This, however, is where too many people form legalistic rules and standards in an attempt to legislate or change a person. But we must always remember that sin is not a behavioral problem, and thus cannot be addressed with behavioral restrictions.

Condemning and rebuking Snyder in the name of love and mercy, making Snyder feel worthless and ashamed because he may smoke cigarettes or still have a beer or two with his friends, will never effect permanent change. In fact, condemnation and rebuke over such actions only increases the shame and guilt in Snyder's life. How could he draw closer to God in loving relationship if he felt separated and distanced from Him by his unworthiness? Guilt and shame hardens the heart, clogs the arteries, and may cause a rejection of God.

Remember that *sin is an outward manifestation of an inward problem.* Perhaps the problem *is* the sin that comes out of a hardened and unrepentant heart. This is easy to see, because the person who commits a sin out of a calloused heart is deliberate in his or her actions. The sin seems to be a part of who the person is; the person identifies with it, because he or she cannot identify with God. The hardened heart thus leaks and manifests through the flesh.

Discern and Deal with Sin

When born-again Christians sin, it is foreign to them – foreign to their spirit. Often it will appear unnatural to those who see it, and it will definitely feel unnatural to those involved in the sin. Let me emphasize, *sin is unnatural to a Christian.* As Christians, we are aliens in this land of sin, foreigners in a land of evil. Yet we still sin. Why? How does that affect us? How can we become more like Christ, the One who never sinned? Look at Matthew 6:24, where Jesus spoke of two masters:

> *No one can serve two masters; for either he will hate the one and love the other, or else he will be loyal to the one and despise the other… (Matthew 6:24 NKJV)*

Though He referenced money being a master, what He is saying is, "Whom do you serve, and where is your heart?" We cannot serve two masters; we cannot be double-minded.

When a Christian does commit a particular sin, he hates it and is remorseful for the sin in his life, because sin is no longer his master. To understand better how sin affects the life of a Christian, peer into the life of the one who called himself "the chief of sinners."

Apostle Paul, probably the greatest evangelist in the history of the world, admitted that he did the things he did not want to do, and did not do the very things he knew he should do. His true love for the Christ he never physically met is a stellar example for all of us today, but still he admits he falls to temptation. Although sin no longer controlled him as his master, sin was still present in his life. This grieved the apostle, it grieved Snyder, and it should grieve anyone who has genuinely and humbly given his or her heart to Jesus. Thank God for His enduring mercy and grace toward us.

You Gotta Die (to Sin)

A Sunday school teacher asked her class what had to happen for a person to go to heaven.

"You have to be a good person. And, you have do good things for people," little Sally exclaimed.

"You have to ask Jesus to forgive you of your sins," said Tommy.

"I know! I know!" blurted Sammy, "You have to be baptized, and then you can go to heaven."

Finally, a shy girl from the back of the class timidly raised her hand.

"Go ahead, Sabrina. Tell us. What must you do in

order to get to heaven?"

"Well," the little girl replied, "You gotta die."

You have to die. A simple answer, but it holds great truth. We must die to our sinful nature and the old "man." The great news of the Gospel is that once you have been born again as a Christian, you are literally dead to sin.

Dead.

When my son Kelton was about two-and-a-half years old, a family of kittens and their mother took up residence on our front porch. Only one kitten, the scrawny orange one, "Tiger," would allow Kelton to pet him, so Tiger naturally became his favorite.

One day, Kelton went out to play with the kitty, but it wouldn't move.

"Daddy, Tiger's batteries are dead." He looked to me for a solution.

Trust me -- batteries wouldn't have revived Tiger. He was as dead and lifeless as can be.

If you are a Christian, the power of sin is as dead as can be in your life. Sin has no life in your life. You are dead to it; you are not slave to it, because all of your answers are found in Christ Jesus. He is the answer to sin. If Jesus Christ lives in you, then you possess the solution to overcoming sin. So, why are you or anyone else still struggling with sin, and the condemnation that follows, if you are dead to sin, and Christ the solution lives in you?

Our buddy Snyder was in the same situation. He lived his life, although now a Christian, as if he were still a sinner headed for the pits of hell. His guilt and shame overtook his very soul with a suffocating grip. He struggled and then battled with condemnation every day. His problem? He wasn't dead enough.

How Dead?

How dead is dead enough? There has to be a corpse, and it has to be handled according to the Word of God! Absorb the following truth in your spirit. Paul admitted his struggle with sin in a most transparent way, but he uncovered more, as we can see in Romans 7:15-25:

> *If, then, I do what I will not to do, I agree with the law that it is good. But now, it is no longer I who do it, but sin that dwells in me. For I know that in me (that is, in my flesh) nothing good dwells; for to will is present with me, but how to perform what is good I do not find. For the good that I will to do, I do not do; but the evil I will not to do, that I practice. Now if I do what I will not to do, it is no longer I who do it, but sin that dwells in me. I find then a law, that evil is present with me, the one who wills to do good. For I delight in the law of God according to the inward man. But I see another law in my members, warring against the law of my mind, and bringing me*

into captivity to the law of sin which is in my members. O wretched man that I am! Who will deliver me from this body of death? I thank God – through Jesus Christ our Lord! So then, with the mind I myself serve the law of God, but with the flesh the law of sin.

Paul was very much like you and me. He struggled with the internal sins of the flesh. Those sins and struggles seem to shower our lives, saturating our flesh with evil thoughts and deeds. What impresses me the most about Paul is that he can be transparent with his struggle. He lets his internal be conflict known to the people whom he oversaw in his ministry. No deceptions here, no chance of being viewed as a hypocrite; and no self-righteous beliefs that would lead to arrogance or pride. Throughout his life and consistently in his writings, Paul showed sincere humility.

Paraphrasing, Paul said: "I'm no longer a slave to sin. I am dead to the very sin that is in my life. I cannot overcome it by my own power. Only by the power of the Holy Spirit in me can I overcome what is in my flesh."

How can you have sin in your life and yet be dead to the sin?

Confusion abounds concerning this. Differing viewpoints on this very matter have divided many churches, ignited many flames of debate, and have surely ushered people into a life and even death without God. Yes, the confusion over sin and the death to sin has misled many -- even people faithfully sitting in pews every Sunday. False deductions have resulted in untruths filtering through congregations all over the world, searing the understanding of multitudes and driving many lost, potential Christians into an eternity of separation from *God*. An eternity. That is *forever without God*. Yikes!

Now a born-again Christian, Snyder was expecting total freedom from his addictions, and from the sinful practices that had kept him in bondage for so many years. He had heard stories of how God's love would free him from addiction, solve his relationship issues, and even help him financially. He should be prosperous in every area, spiritually, emotionally, and financially – rich in the Spirit – yet he saw no evidence. Did he have true salvation, or was it all just an empty promise?

Your Notes:

The "Jesus Life Enhancement" message that many use to draw people to Christ is not biblical. We never see Jesus, or John the Baptist, or anyone in the Bible teaching, "Repent – and God will make your life better!" They preached, "Repent! For the Kingdom of God is at hand."
– Wayne Sutton

Chapter Six

Have I Got A Deal For You!

Old Testament law shows us our need for grace. Its purpose was never to make us righteous, but rather to show us our need for a Savior. Thus, we should bring people to the grace of Jesus Christ for their salvation and for reconciliation with their heavenly Father. However, we must be careful not to use a life-enhancement message as a draw card for salvation. That means we should not offer people a "quick fix" for their life's problems, using the Sinner's Prayer as a "magic talisman."

God is not Aladdin, and the Bible is not a magical lamp; nor should we ever teach such lies and assumptions to a lost and already-dying world. Can God heal, save, recover, and rebuild the damage done by the enemy? Can the God we serve cleanse and purify a putrid and scarred heart? Absolutely. Yet when we promise self-improvement or a life-enhancement message as the only reason to accept Christ, it may set the person up for disappointment and despair when life throws the inevitable curve balls.

"Snyder," such promises might say, "God will take away your desires for drugs. God will heal your depression. God will cancel your debts. God will heal you. God will give you prosperity. God will…God will…" A person may start to think that if he accepts Jesus into his heart, all his problems or challenges will go away, *snap,* just like that. Certainly, God will bless and heal and move in all of those areas -- sometimes by process and sometimes instantly. But the basis for the desire to be saved should be relationship with Christ Jesus, and healing through that relationship.

True Repentance?

If someone makes a decision to accept Christ because of what He can do for him or her, stay close. This person needs true repentance to take hold: encourage the person to seek relationship with Him. Without true repentance, the person has not made a heart decision for Christ. An argument might be that God healed and blessed those whom He saved, according to Bible record. Or that God loves His children, and wants to bless and prosper them. If it is all there, in black and white, what is wrong with offering the promises to those who are struggling with sin or sickness in their lives? God is concerned with salvation, truly concerned about reconciliation back to Him, and that concern is primary over other desires.

Snyder received this revelation one day in frustration as he lamented, "God, why can't You help me overcome? Why aren't You doing what we both know You can do! Why the pain, the suffering?"

God took Snyder back to a time when his Uncle Ray took him squirrel hunting in the mountains. Snyder was only about seven years old at the time. Although his Uncle Ray would not let him hold or fire the rifle, the hunting adventure still made the youngster feel a step closer to manhood. However, the momentary feeling of power and independence shattered when Snyder stumbled over the root of a pine tree and tumbled headlong into a small creek. Uncle Ray raced to his aid. Blood gushed in a fountain from his nephew's neck where the jagged edge of the root gashed his jugular. Ray applied pressure to the wide-open wound, scooped him up, and tore through the woods to the car, and straight to an emergency room.

When they arrived at the hospital, Snyder had already lost a lot of blood. The nurses and a surgeon assessed him quickly and rushed him into the operating room in an attempt to save his life.

"You'll be okay," the nurse said, seeing Snyder stir just before they hooked up the IV to put him under. But he seemed agitated about something and raised his hand up for them to see.

"Doctor…"

"I'll fix you up – you'll be just fine," assured the surgeon, ignoring the hand to concentrate on the neck.

"Doctor!" Snyder called, waving his finger side-to-side.

"Look at the big splinter in my finger!"

The doctor wasn't as concerned as Snyder was about removing the splinter. First, he had to deal with the life-threatening neck wound. But to Snyder, the splinter was a big deal, because he couldn't see what the surgeon saw.

"I'll take care of it, I promise, once we fix your neck."

Decades later, Snyder was still in the figurative woods, the same hospital room, and holding up the same bloodied finger with the splinter in it, as many are.

"God, please take away my drug habit."
"Please heal my arthritis."
"Please handle my debt."
"Please God, remove the splinter!"

But God...It Hurts!

However, many people are still in the creek, dying. God sees His children there, lying lifeless and in despair, crimson with sin. He has to save us, bring us to life, and only then can the process of removing the splinter begin.

Where is your creek? What jagged branch has severed your life? And what splinters are you holding up to God? Yes, God can remove our splinters; but His priorities are set upon our salvation and reconciliation first. So should Snyder, and everyone else for that matter, seek God for help in his or her day-to-day problems? Yes. The Bible tells us to be anxious over nothing, yet pray about everything. We should pray about our debt, about our health, about any addictions or unwanted habits -- and we should pray about our sins. We should always pray. Just remember to examine yourself and your heart and ensure that the jugular has been repaired before you focus on the splinter. In other words, God sees the greater need, and until that is dealt with, splinter repair might not happen.

The "Jesus Life Enhancement" message that many use to draw people to Christ is not biblical. We never see Jesus or John the Baptist, or anyone else in the Bible teaching, "Repent – and God will make your life better!" They preached "Repent! For the Kingdom of God is at hand. Repent, for there is a day of judgment coming, a day of either glory for those who are born again, or a day of frightful horrors for those who have not accepted Christ as their personal Savior."

Many well-intentioned people believe they should do anything it takes to get a person saved. But that is *not* God's way.

"Snyder, God will take away your drug addiction!" sounds like a great promise. But what happens to Snyder when the urge to grab another pill or smoke another joint hounds him?

"Snyder, God will take away your sexual addiction!" Again, a seemingly great draw card – until his fiancée's flesh comes up against his own.

"Snyder, God will bless you and take away your debts!" Tell that to the landlord or the credit card company, when he's run out of money before the bills were paid.

If Snyder's salvation experience were built on a foundation of life-enhancement promises, and if healing failed to manifest in his areas of difficulty – would he then doubt his salvation? Would he lose trust and respect towards those who told him about Christ? Worse still, would he now doubt God? Broken promises lead to broken trust, and that reparation process is a challenge.

Many, many Christians come to Christ via the life-enhancement message. Perhaps you did. If so, how did it make you feel, or, how do you feel now, if the promises have not lined up with your present troubles or trials?

It is vital for us to follow the *biblical model* of evangelism, and teach salvation based on true repentance and reconciliation with Christ. That is the purpose of the Law: to show us our need for a savior, to show us our need for Jesus Christ. Thus, when a person accepts Christ as payment for his or her sins, his or her spirit is reborn and is truly dead to sin. The person is no longer a sinner trying to become righteous through works, but a reborn

Christian. Although he might be afflicted in the flesh or mind, he is a reborn spirit who can now find transformation. Selah!

Your Notes:

"Transparency is breaking the masquerade of perfection that we attempt to show to the world. The Bible tells us to be holy, so we believe that we must portray a view of holiness, an act of holiness toward others. The problem is not in our desire to be holy, but in our attempt to portray an image of holiness. This not only hurts us, but also is a huge obstacle for the lost in need of a Savior."

– Wayne Sutton

Chapter Seven

Transparency for Transformation

"Hello, Snyder, my name is Jenny." This was the start of a beautiful friendship, in many ways.

Jenny was Snyder's co-worker, and a former drug addict and alcoholic herself. And Jenny was the only person in his life who was able to reach him with the truth about the transforming power of the *true* Gospel of Jesus Christ. She had been to the creek; and in fact was still in it in many ways, even after inviting Jesus into her life. But she was confident of who she was in Him, in spite of herself, unlike Snyder. Splinters yet remained, but the very core of her being -- her heart -- was undergoing transformation.

Jenny understood where Snyder was coming from. She herself had asked the same questions after she invited Christ into her heart. She was saved while serving time at the rehab center, when she attended some Bible studies. However, in the absence of a preacher or a church, she had to find most of her answers on her own. Though saved, she really didn't understand it all, and had a lot of questions.

"Who really *is* this Jesus? What is sin? Is God really here to help us, or is He a distant deity who leaves us alone to fight and claw our way to the top rung of the ladder of life? What if…what if there is a *chance* that God does care…that He can help me change?"

Questions are good! God loves seekers! Seek His

tutelage! By and by, Jenny found herself reading the Bible more, becoming more and more drawn to it. While before, it would lie on her nightstand untouched for days, now hardly a day could pass without Jenny searching the Book for the answers her heart sought.

Jenny did not always understand what she read; some of it made no sense at all. For example: what is redemption? Sanctification? Justification? Jenny knew that the Word claimed the Man Jesus to be not only her Savior, Friend, Healer, Deliverer, Lord, and King, but also the answer to her problems. Her quest for knowledge compelled her to pore over its pages. There were times she couldn't seem to put the Book down.

Yes, the Truth drew her in to discover the answers for herself, devoid of manmade notions and interpretations, such that one day she finally grasped the mystery we call "salvation." She knew with conviction that she had accepted Christ, not by her own actions, but by faith in Him and in His promises. She was saved *with* all of her baggage. She was not any less saved if she still found addiction a struggle, or even if she slipped. Jenny was *growing* in Christ. It was a process. She may have not looked the part of a traditional member of an upright church, she may not have even acted the part -- but she was not any less saved.

A Little or a Lot Saved?

Sadly, so many in the Church today view someone's outward appearance or actions, and immediately judge- "That person cannot know Christ: no way is that person going to heaven!" They judge and condemn someone based on their own view of morality or personal set of rules, either put there by the Church, or self-imposed.

If Jenny were to walk into their church, they would probably tell her she needed Christ. What would that do to Jenny, who had already accepted Jesus as her Savior and was going through that growth and maturation process? Jesus accepted her as she was, with all of her frailty and weakness. She sought Jesus, and invited Him into her heart; and now, people tell her He has not been there all along? How is she expected to grow if people keep telling her that she hasn't got the foundation yet? What if they tell her she hasn't yet found The Answer whom she believed to *be* The Answer, who would love and accept her unconditionally as she was, and help her grow? Jenny would feel very much deserted and lied to. Some have the best intentions, but are misdirected. They need to get into the Word as Jenny did, to discover the truth for themselves.

Jenny met Snyder three years into her salvation experience. It had been a process for her; she had fought many of the same demons that Snyder now faced in his walk. Every day, the silent screams of addiction taunted her. The scars of a heart broken too often sometimes lured her into unhealthy relationships. The enemy tried to take advantage every time she was down by making her heart grow sick through dashed hopes: "Hope deferred makes a heart grow sick." But that didn't mean she wasn't saved. And that's what Snyder needed to hear. Until he met Jenny and saw her transparency, he would struggle.

Identifying the "Untils"

"Hello, Snyder, my name is Jenny." This was Snyder's "until" moment. I remember a pastor once telling me that I would one day meet my own "until" person. He explained that many people are under the influence and captivity of a religious spirit, blinded by a veil of deception, until they have an encounter with their "until" person. An "until" person is that one man or woman with the divine ability to reach another man or woman with spiritual truths. Jenny was predestined to be Snyder's "until" person.

"Hello, Jenny, nice to meet you," was the start of a predestined, eternal relationship ordained by a heavenly Father who loves His children, and who desires to see that His children know the truth that can really set them free.

Getting to know Jenny was an eye-opening, epiphanal experience for Snyder in his personal walk with the Lord.

The Real Deal

"Transparency is one of the crucial keys to changing your life," Jenny told Snyder. Transparency is breaking the masquerade of perfection that we attempt to portray to the world. The Bible tells us to be holy, so we believe that we must portray a view of holiness, an act of holiness toward others. The problem is not in our desire to be holy, but in our attempt to portray an image of holiness. This not only hurts us but also is a huge obstacle for the lost in need of a Savior.

"When I look at the other Christians at my church and at work, they seem to be so perfect. They seem so happy, so full of joy, and I never see any problems in their life. I never experience the life they are living. What's wrong with my salvation?" Snyder sincerely asked Jenny. "What now?"

Playing the masquerade game, which is trying to *appear* perfect and righteous in one's own flesh, actually goes against the very Word of God. When Snyder attempted to live the holy masquerade through his flesh, he failed. His shortcomings and failures contrasted sharply when compared to the canvas of the religious show his fellow Christians displayed.

I struggled with this in my life for years before I grasped the truth that truly set me free. It was a pattern developed with the hope of obtaining perfect holiness and living righteously daily. I would start my mornings filled with petitions for God, asking Him to help me maintain the holiness people expected of a Christian. "Lord, please help me live a righteous life today. Help me keep my language clean, my thoughts pure, that I might always be a witness for You. Amen."

Kiss Despair-Filled Days Good-bye

The evening prayer was a little less upbeat and usually lined with fear, encased with doubt and discouragement. "Lord, forgive me, I have failed yet again. My heart wasn't always in the right place today, and my thoughts not always pure. I did not witness either. I am so sorry. Please do not hold this against me, and please forgive me of my sins committed today. Amen."

"Today" for Snyder, as it was for me, was often a day of despair, another failed day of hope—the hope of obtaining glory, yet deferred again. *Perhaps tomorrow,* Snyder would think...*maybe tomorrow I can finally please God and get to some level of righteousness.*

How many of us pray these condemning and self-defeating prayers? Hope deferred makes a heart grow sick. Sick! I felt sick when I could not live up to that level of righteousness and that image of holiness. Snyder felt sick in heart, so much that he questioned his salvation. *Am I really saved? Have I been born again? Is this Christianity?*

How many times will Snyder have to question the finished work of the cross? How often will he question his own worthiness before he turns his back on the Church, and ultimately on Jesus Christ Himself?

I speak as one who knows – and I am being as transparent to you as Jenny was with Snyder. Self-condemnation and guilt had eroded my heart so that I often questioned my own salvation. I even believed that I could never live up to the lifestyle, and I was not worthy enough to call myself a Christian. Soon, I tired of even trying to be one, and in frustration, walked away from the Church, and eventually away from the Lord. "You are a backslider," the religious folk said, feeding me even more condemnation, reasons to feel guilty. "You turned away from the Church and God and you are in danger of hell!" Feeling a lot less love and a whole lot more condemnation, I sank back into my world of sin, fraught with despair and hopelessness.

"*Until* you recognize who you already are in Christ; *until* you realize your place in the heavenly realm; *until* you can glimpse the finished work of the cross that is manifest within you already, you will never be able to have freedom or transformation from the shell of guilt you are living in," said Jenny. *Until*: there's that word again. It always means something good following, in this case.

I once heard it said that Christianity was like an old mattress. An old mattress may be firm on both ends, but worn out and sagging in the middle. On one end, you are born again, and you experience the true salvation experience! Life is grand! On the other end, you will, one day, face death on this earth, but you get to go to heaven and experience eternal life with God! Life is grand! The problem, however, as with the mattress, is the in-between. In between your salvation experience and the eternity in heaven is a lumpy life of struggles, trials, confusion, pain, and despair. This is the area that many of us live in, Jenny and Snyder as well, searching for the life that we want, but that seems to elude us: peace, purpose, and abundant life.

The Truth about Self-Condemnation

Self-condemnation affects our attitude and our faith. What is it doing there? The Bible tells us that there is no condemnation to those who are in Christ Jesus (see Rom. 8:1) -- none. If you are born again, then you are *in* Christ Jesus, and He is *in* you. You have been crucified with Christ, and it is no longer you who live but Christ who lives in you (see Gal. 2:20). Condemnation is not in you. Jesus is in you. Jesus does not condemn you.

> *"The mystery that has been hidden from ages and from generations, but now has been revealed to His saints. To them God willed to make known what are the riches of the glory of this mystery among the Gentiles:* **which is Christ in you, the hope of glory**. *Him we preach, warning every man and teaching every man in all wisdom, that we may present every man perfect in Christ Jesus." (Colossians 1:26-28, NKJV emphasis mine).*

Christ in you, the hope of glory! When you are saved, your spirit is reborn, your spirit is made new and alive, and you are at that very moment made righteous and blameless before the Lord! Your salvation is surely complete, and you are a new creation! This point is where most Christians miss their blessings and inheritance, allowing the enemy to destroy their lives. The lies from the very pits of hell have invaded our religious institutions and brought with them the demons of guilt and condemnation to attack our souls and flesh.

"You missed the mark, Snyder. You are not righteous in the least," whispers the enemy. "You sinned again. Jenny and God will surely hold that sin against you," the serpent assures. "You failed again, and God must be getting tired of hearing your same excuses every night you pray. HE IS A GOD OF WRATH and His WRATH will SURELY FALL upon your life."

***

"No!" insisted Jenny, when Snyder confided his struggles and discouragement. "You are already righteous, you are blameless, and God accepted you! You were made complete by the sacrifice of Jesus, and not by your own good works."

We ignore and even overlook the finished work of the cross when we attempt to earn our own salvation by the keeping of a set doctrine of laws and regulations. Paul faced the same dilemma over two thousand years ago, with the church in Galatia. Recall earlier when Paul called them "foolish," and said, *"Who has bewitched you?"* (Gal. 3:1). Nothing has changed from then until now. They needed to receive Christ by faith and through the grace of a loving God to be saved, rather than try to maintain their salvation by external works, rules, and regulations.

We may not feel complete: neither righteous nor holy, especially when our thoughts and actions do not mirror His image. But does that make us incomplete? Some teachings in the Church say yes. Some say no. The answer lies in knowing and understanding your makeup.

Your Notes:

"And the very God of peace sanctify you wholly; and I pray God your whole spirit and soul and body be preserved blameless unto the coming of our Lord Jesus Christ."
(1 Thessalonians 5:23 NKJV).

Chapter Eight

Reprogram Your Consciousness

Some people believe that they consist of only body and soul, and others believe that the body and soul are one. This is a primary reason why people hold themselves and others in the suffocating grip of condemnation. A proper understanding of who you are will actually help you step away from condemnation and guilt, and free you to praise God during your experiences of transformation and change.

> *"Now may the God of peace Himself sanctify you completely; and may your whole <u>spirit, soul,</u> and <u>body</u> be preserved blameless at the coming of our Lord Jesus Christ"* (1 Thessalonians 5:23 NKJV Emphasis mine).

When you accept Christ as your Lord and Savior, then your spirit is reborn, and you now have a new spirit within you. This spiritual transformation is complete; the finished work of the cross brings about the change. Your soul and your body, however, are separate and different from your spirit. These first two areas are where the true battlegrounds lie, and where we find countless casualties. The battles that we all must face are practically inevitable, yet the casualties do not have to occur in this battle, once we understand the differences in the body, soul, and spirit.

Jenny began to capture this truth while a relatively new Christian, still participating heavily in the party life with her friends and co-workers. She had accepted Christ during her time in the rehabilitation center; yet very shortly after she was sent back home, she found herself plunging back into the party life and destructive behavior once again. Sometimes it was drinking one too many beers with her friends and passing out on the floor of the bathroom, and sometimes it was allowing someone to get too intimate and quickly diving back into a night of sexual gratification. Drugs, alcohol, sex, and the daily uncontrollable impure thoughts seemed to flow naturally as part of her life. Thus her question: "Why would a Christian fall right back into a life of sin?"

Studying the Scriptures, she saw in Thessalonians that she was not only flesh, and not only spirit, but instead was actually *three* separate parts living as *one* being. Spirit, soul, and flesh are all part of Jenny, yet all three are different as well.

You are three different forms within one identity known as you! Your flesh is your literal body that you see as you peer into a mirror. This flesh can go forth and produce sins, can be harmed, and can even do good works; but the flesh only follows the direction of the soul. Theologians label our soul as the *mental aspects of our lives*. Your emotions, your thought processes, and your will are all parts of your soul. This also becomes confusing for too many Christians, new or mature in their faith. Your soul will surely affect the actions and reactions of your flesh, as you take your daily walk through the valleys and mountains of life.

The soulish realm is where Snyder was having his battle. The wounds from that battle were affecting his spiritual walk, and the condition of his flesh. Feeling as though he had failed God by his struggles and temptations of the soulish realm, he believed this area was damning his spiritual walk with Christ. This self-defeating belief system only made it easier for him to plunge back deeper into the sins of the flesh, causing destruction and harm to reign in his life.

The spirit is spirit and the flesh is flesh; the two are not the same. The Bible tells us that we must worship God in *spirit* and in *truth*. There is a difference between spirit and truth, too! Sins of the flesh are actually *outward* manifestations of an inward problem. The lying, stealing, cursing, and other "typical" sins are brought to life by the inward problem of a sinful nature and sinful programming.

When you accept Christ as your Savior, your spirit is not changed; but your spirit literally exchanges with the Spirit of Christ. Your years, or even decades, of programming in a lifestyle of sin, however, will still take time to reprogram. Society and your environment are always programming the divinely-inspired computer between your ears, and hence you act according to the programming within. The brain, or the soulish realm, as the Bible calls it, is not instantly transformed when you are born again. We must renew our mind daily with the fresh teachings of the Word of God to reprogram our consciousness, and ultimately bring healing to our damaged life.

***

"Good magazine?" asked Jenny sarcastically, rolling her eyes for emphasis, as Snyder thumbed through the latest swimsuit edition of his favorite sports magazine.

"Yeah," he muttered, his face reddening. "It sure is hard to be a Christian sometimes. Why don't these stupid thoughts go away?"

"Junk in, junk out," said Jenny. "Remember, you are *feeding* the soul and the flesh with that stuff."

"Now you're getting legalistic on me!"

"I'm not being legalistic, Snyder, just telling you the facts."

"What facts? The *thou shalt not* facts?

"Nope," she replied, "...*the fact* that what we bring into the realm of our minds does affect us, good or bad. The Bible teaches this very thing! It tells us that we are not to conform to the world, but be transformed by the renewing of our mind, so that we can prove what God's will is, what is good, acceptable, and perfect."[1] His Word also tells us that we are to keep ourselves from being polluted by the world.[2]

"How do you say no to temptation, Snyder? How do you get rid of those plaguing thoughts? By cleansing your mind! And that requires a daily renewing, a daily filling of your mind with the things of God: His Word (reading the Bible), prayer (discussions with God), worship (singing

---

1 See Romans 12:2.
2 See James 1:27.

and praise), and listening to His precious Holy Spirit.

"The more of God you put in that noggin of yours, the less space for temptation and wrong desires," she said, gesturing with her head in the direction of his magazine.

"Why not trade your magazine time, or some other time you spending doing stuff that feeds your mind garbage, for God-time? Why don't you trade it for the transforming presence and knowledge of Christ in your life? I guarantee, my friend, that your desire for God-things will increase, and your desire for the things of the world will decrease!"

Snyder had much to contemplate, but it made sense. Jenny eventually made headway, and Snyder began to understand that the battle truly was in his mind.

***

Years of programming and our sinful nature influence the Body of Christ, too. "Casualties" have abounded for too long; the lies of hell have haunted and damned people for generations. It is time for Christians to experience victory in the battle for the mind. *"For the wages of sin is death..."* (Romans 6:23). One act of sin can open the gates of hell and destruction; it can open doorways for the "wages" to creep in. Denying sin and opting to renew our mind slams the door shut on the enemy, closing off his avenue of death.

Is this legalism? No. This is not about trying to earn the love God by following a set of rules or laws. It is about our responsibility to renew and reprogram our consciousness so that we might live as victors. God tells us to renew our minds daily because He loves us, and wants to work through our life bringing forth victory in body, soul, and spirit.

Your Notes:

"It is finished."
– Jesus Christ from John 19:30

Chapter Nine

Faith in the Positive Power

Only one name can destroy the works of the devil: Jesus, the Name above all names. Giant of faith Smith Wigglesworth said, "Even the best thought of holiness must be on the decrease, in order that Christ may *increase.*" The enemy's *primo tacto* is to persuade you to deny the name and power of Jesus! There is power in the name of Jesus! All power, all authority, yes! Why, then, are Christians perishing? Why are they backsliding, falling away? Because of a lack of knowledge,[3] a deep-down conviction, that in Christ is all power and all authority, and that Satan has no hold on us. Christians perish for lack of knowledge. We believe on the outside, but show no belief in our actions or attitudes. Do we actually walk in that place of power and authority?

***

"Why is the enemy so effective in his attacks against me?" Snyder asked Jenny, as he leafed through a nearby Bible. "Everywhere I read in this Book tells me something different. There are promises of victory and overcoming power...so then why do I struggle so? I have mountains of junk yet to overcome. The enemy has it over me for sure."

"Stop giving the devil so much credit!" rebuked Jenny. "You are glorifying him by your words and your defeatist attitude, and it has to stop. Try speaking of what

---
[3] See Hosea 4:6.

God has done, is doing, and can and will do. How about, 'The enemy has no hold over me. I can do all things through Christ, who gives me strength. Yea, though I walk through the valley of the shadow of death, I will fear no evil, because He is with me....' You know, glorify God and His strength and His power."

In His Name...

Snyder had more faith in the negative power of Satan than he did in the divine power of God. He needed to bring forth and to remember the truth and fact of God's love and power. Christ said it Himself: that *all* authority had been given to Him, both in heaven and in earth, and He has given this authority to us, the believers. [4]

"All" is a powerful word when partnered with "authority," which in the Greek translation is *exousia,* meaning "delegated authority." *"In His name, [we] will cast out demons...!"* (see Mark 16:17). We are to use the authority that He has delegated and entrusted to us, to overcome the works of evil. "In His name" *is the key* to *unlocking the power of God* in our lives. "In His name" equips us to overcome enslaving realms of darkness and spiritual battles.

The apostle Paul knew well that our weapons are not carnal, but are *mighty through God* to the pulling down of strongholds.

"For the weapons of our warfare are not physical [weapons of flesh and blood],

---
4 See Matthew 28:18

but they are mighty before God for the overthrow and destruction of strongholds, [Inasmuch as we] refute arguments and theories and reasonings and every proud and lofty thing that sets itself up against the [true] knowledge of God; and we lead every thought and purpose away captive into the obedience of Christ (the Messiah, the Anointed One)" (2 Corinthians 10:4,5 AMP).

The mind is a battlefield. In the battlefield are strongholds, unhealthy – even deadly – ways of thinking that can keep us captive or lead us into captivity. It is ongoing spiritual warfare: the need to daily renew our minds and employ the weapon and authority of Jesus' name to overcome.

We give credit to the enemy for always holding us captive, always attacking us as soon as we seem to stand up, and for always being one step ahead of our deliverance. In actuality, the problem is usually a stronghold, a seemingly endless spiritual valley we have found ourselves to be walking through. The solution to exiting this valley of pain and struggle is to use the delegated authority we already possess.

"It is finished." – Jesus Christ [5]

Three words spoken by the One who holds *all* authority. It is accomplished. It is finished. It is done. A *fait accompli*. Oh, if only we could finally understand the finished work of the cross and how it applies to our entire life, now and in eternity!

[5] See John 19:30.

Why does the enemy, therefore, so often succeed in holding us back, when we, each one of us, hold the very Name, and therefore, the authority of Jesus Christ? Because we believe the deadly whispers, the spoon-fed lies, thus permitting the enemy to work where he has no right to work! We focus our eyes upon the sin and its wages instead of on Christ, the Atonement.

Exalt Not the Devil!

It is okay to be full of faith, to be full of faith in the Word and the promises of God, and speak them! Stop giving the devil center stage! Oh, the devil made me do it...I can't help this sin...I can't get well...the devil is attacking my children...The devil this and the devil that. Exalt and lift up the power of God, please! No wonder we have generations of believers living in despair and sickness. No wonder the churches are void of miracles. We have faith -- gobs of it; but it's misdirected faith. We fully expect the devil to keep his end of the deal, bringing death, finality, and destruction to lives. Yet we beg God, "Just help me survive...so that I don't suffer too much."

What a dim, dim view, in a dimmer light! We are not survivors! We don't have to exist or survive, or hang by a thread. It is finished. We are victors. We have authority. We have power. Be faithful with it.

Faithful with the Authority

"His lord said unto him, 'Well done, good and faithful servant, you have been

> *faithful over a few things, I will make you ruler over many things…'" (Matthew 25:23 NKJV)*

We must learn to be faithful with the authority God has given us, as believers. When we start taking action, and speaking forth truth into our lives, and claiming the victory that Christ has provided for us, then God will reward us with even more. It is my belief that once we are faithful in praying and speaking, in the authority that has already been given to us, then God faithfully gives us *more* authority and more power, to accomplish even more. We are still asking God for power when we have failed to be faithful with the very authority He has already bestowed unto us. Jesus Christ said that it is finished: have faith that it is so.

***

"No one understands me! How can God understand the hell I go through every single day?" snapped Snyder. As their friendship grew, the conversations became more and more centered on God. Sometimes Jenny had an answer, and sometimes not. However, their exchanges, at the same time as they helped her friend, taught her to rely on the leadership and guidance of the Holy Spirit for wisdom.

In this case, Jenny knew that God truly understood Snyder, just as He understood her, as He understands us. We can expect God to sympathize with us. Hebrews 4:15 reminds us that Christ understands our struggles and trials because He encountered them Himself, and was tempted in all points – all points! Yet without sin.

Jesus Christ faced what you are facing, He faced what you have already faced, and He faced everything you will ever face about temptation. He can sympathize with you, with me, with Snyder, and with anyone facing a temptation today.

What ones are you battling? Are they knock, knock, knocking on the door of your mind? Some temptations are not obvious; you may not recognize something as harmful. But the devil is sleek and cunning, stealthy and creepy. He'll subtly make you think it is all okay. Are you given to greed, slander, gossip, self-righteousness, pride, over-indulging? The devil works diligently to set up strongholds in your mind; and he does so through strategy and deceit, deliberate, well-thought-out, targeted deception, preying on your weaknesses. And he is in no hurry, taking his time to work his plan. This is why something might not be so obvious.

Just remember, Jesus faced what you are facing. He sympathizes with you, and relates to your temptations. The Name above all Names will lead you not into temptation, He will deliver you from it. Sickness, depression, despair, temptation must bow down to Jesus. Do not let the spirit of anti-Christ, which by the way is alive and working even in the Body of Christ, nullify the power and authority given to you.

Your Notes:

"Hope deferred makes the heart grow sick. Hope deferred erodes faith. Hope deferred causes people to walk away from their churches, and from God. If you are on this treadmill, get off it right now. Uncover the truth of the finished work of the cross, and find rest in the Lord."

– Wayne Sutton

Chapter Ten

Cross-Works vs. Cross Walks

The one truth you must realize to receive effective transformation is a major tenet of orthodox Christianity: Jesus Christ made atonement for your sins, and His work on the cross is the only work that is required. Your faith in His work appropriates His grace. Everything you need has been given to you in the finished work of the cross. Don't overlook, forget, gloss over, or fail to acknowledge this transforming work, and the gift of His power; of the Holy Spirit who lives within you.

You may come up against deception in the guise of religion: a package wrapped in holiness and self-righteousness. Satan, as I mentioned, is the father of lies, often subtle. He will even use church leaders to advance his agenda and make you believe that your works determine your salvation. He attempts to destroy the effectiveness of your witness by engaging his demonic army to veil or hide the full effect of the finished work. That is where the battle begins.

So many are deceived; and we, as brothers and sisters in Christ, are hurting each other, as we give in to the lies of the devil. And he is cunning. He knows, for the most part, that we wouldn't believe him if he told us that God did not love us, or that He thought us worthless, that we were all hell-bound. So he pretties it up and makes his lies sound holy and righteous, and we grab hold of them, as truth. Sadly, often even the unbeliever swallows the lie as truth, believing that he or she is not good enough for God to save.

"But I was a *good* person," says the person crying out from the pit of damnation. This person believed the lie that morality was the way to heaven, thus diminishing the finished work of the cross.

Snyder was in that place once, as a not-yet-believer. "I don't hurt or cheat people, and I always give what I can to charity. I don't have to go to church to go to heaven," he countered his friend Tom, who had shared the Gospel with him.

The Morality Equation

The Bible tells us that individuals will call themselves, and regard themselves as, "good people." This belief is only cemented deeper into such a person's lost soul, as he or she views performance-based religions. Such religions reward (even if only verbally) those who do good deeds, and condemn and ridicule those who do what they consider to be evil.

The view of morality equaling salvation stretches among other religions and cultures as well. The cause and effect (if I do good I get rewarded) belief spills over to the Muslim's Koran, the Buddhist's belief, and virtually every culture known to man, in and out of religion. A person's promotion at work is usually performance-based. A child achieving learning outcomes advances to the next grade. Animals are not exempt. If the dog behaves, Rover gets his reward. If we are good, we will get to heaven.

The question then becomes, how good is good? What is the "goodness criterion" to get to heaven? Do we rate it as we would a restaurant, in terms of sanitation? Do we base it on letter grades as in school? "Oh, let's see," says God. "You just slipped in with a C-minus."

I recall my report cards in grade school, especially bringing them home to judge and jury a.k.a. Mom and Dad. Good grades yielded reward, and bad grades - well, punishment until the next report.

So if God went by the report card or grading method, how would you score? How good do you have to be? What letter grade gets us into heaven? What is good enough? An A+, perhaps a B? Anything below that meant punishment for me. Heaven help us all if we get a D or an F. How good is good enough, and how bad is too bad? If we are supposed to merit salvation by performance, why doesn't the Bible give us such criteria, such rules and parameters?

Some people argue that it does, referring to the Bible as The Rule Book, pointing us in the direction of Levitical law and the Ten Commandments. But without the power of the Holy Spirit working in and through us, without exercising and walking in the authority given to us by the Lord Jesus Christ, we will fail in meeting those expectations.

Beware the Pervading Spirit of Legalism!

I was raised in a very legalistic Pentecostal church, which I still love and respect. However, I just could not agree with all their teachings, bound by the Law. Even as a child, I knew the rules were not lining up with my spirit. The church was growing, people were being saved and receiving Christ into their hearts, and we saw actual miracles and manifestations of God that would shock and amaze most Christians today. We saw the power of God work through His people but we also saw the spirit of legalism and self-righteousness at work. "You have to be holy," we were told; so we tried.

"You have to be perfect," we were told, so we tried. Our church, as so many others, had its own set of rules and regulations set forth specifically to gauge another person's salvation or their "worthiness" to be a member of our establishment.

I can tell of so many sermons that lashed out against the "sins" of tobacco use, alcohol consumption, and even the "sin" of wearing make-up or jewelry. Wow! *Many people must be going to hell,* I thought as a child. I once remember a young guy who testified to the entire congregation, how disgusted he was when he saw that someone had worn a cross as an earring. He actually boasted that he wanted to snatch it, rip it from the person's ear in defense of the name of Jesus. Everyone agreed with collective "amens" and votes of approval for his legalistic self-righteousness. Sad. Whatever happened to the apostle Paul's warning, *"Let no man tell you what you can touch, taste, or handle...."*

According to my church, if someone didn't lay down an offensive addiction, garment, piece of jewelry or the like, he or she would be damned to hell. It was proof he or she was not born again.

Snyder felt damned. I felt damned at times. Many today feel damned. It is a lose/lose situation in such a church where one feels damned in it because of the self-righteous teachings of judgment, and damned for being out of it, a sure signal of a backslider. Sad that they base what type of Christian you are or are not on a level of personal outward holiness, measured against manmade standards.

Based on these standards, I was not "good enough" and I eventually grew weary of trying. Sure, during the occasional revivals I felt forgiven again; and maybe during a Sunday evening altar call I could shed enough tears to "pray through" for forgiveness. But I felt that somehow I lost the victory and lost my salvation once again, somewhere between the altar on Sunday and the front door walking back in the next Sunday morning. How holy was holy enough to make heaven my home?

Rules Can Kill You

If good deeds improve my score and bad deeds or sins deduct from my score, then why didn't God make the rules and the scoring system a lot easier to find in the Bible? Where are the rules that I am suppose to live by, be judged by, and will perish or be rewarded by? How awful not to know for sure if I will make it to heaven, no matter how hard I try to be a good person, or do my best!

***

"What kind of God would make His rules so hard to understand, never set out specific expectations, never tell me what I needed to achieve, and then send me to hell for failing?" *Perhaps,* thought Snyder, *it would be easier to accept my life as hell on earth and give up trying to be a Christian. I always fail miserably.*

These were cries of his heart, cries of "Help me, God. I don't understand. I want to serve You, but…I try, but…"

Jenny understood. She could relate to Snyder and to his challenges in understanding the heart of God, and his frustrations that he couldn't please God. Nor could he change. Jenny had to seek the truth for herself before she could truly understand. This is something each one of us has to do, Snyder too. The truth is in the Word of God, and the Holy Spirit will reveal it to us each uniquely.

Jenny tried to assure Snyder, nevertheless. "You will never be good enough of your own self; it can't be done!" Her words cut deep into his heart…*never good enough….* "What in hell does *that* mean?"

"You are never *of yourself* going to be good enough; you can never grade high enough; and you will never pass the 'make it into heaven' test on your own merits, morality, or good works. But it's a blessing…understand? If you were able to earn your salvation based on your works or your moral understanding, you'd lose it, partner! Me too! Time to face the reality. You will never measure up. You are only saved by the blood sacrifice of Jesus Christ. Only then can you rest in your salvation, only then can you truly appreciate the One who has set you free. Only then can you truly love Jesus with all your heart!"

Step off the Treadmill

Are you living on this treadmill of despair and hope deferred? Are you one of the millions of people who go throughout life wondering, *Am I ready? Am I truly born-again? Am I worthy? Will I see heaven one day, or will I bust hell wide open as God rejects me?* If you had to rely on your good works to somehow outweigh the evil or bad works, how would you know when enough is enough? How would you know for sure you were forgiven of every sin you committed through your daily walk, if you alone were responsible?

We awaken and pray with every good intention: "Father, help me not to sin today, help me keep myself clean, and not to sin against You…" Then we get out into our day, and we sin. Why? We are supposed to be dead to sin, and yet we struggle with it. Paul struggled. Yes, he was a man of God, with loads of faith, but he lamented all the same. He wanted not to sin, but did. At night, after our day of disappointment, we breathe forth another prayer. It, too, is well meaning, but usually results in self-condemnation or guilt. "Father, I messed up. I tried not to sin. I said things I shouldn't have said to someone. I thought things that were impure. I lusted. Forgive me, God. Please forgive me."

Sounds humble enough: but really listen next time for that undertone of condemnation. If it starts with you and ends with you, it usually is. How many "I's" are in your prayer? I messed up. I sinned. I fell short. Where is

God and the finished work of the cross in that prayer? Hey, Snyder prayed like that for years but it only persuaded him more of his unworthiness, separating him from God, creating a gulf, and causing despair that he would ever measure up as a disciple.

Hope deferred makes the heart grow sick. Hope deferred erodes faith. Hope deferred causes people to walk away from their churches, and from God. If you are on this treadmill, get off it right now. Uncover the truth of the finished work of the cross, and find rest in the Lord.

Jenny shared with Snyder the fact that a person will never 'know' God through rules and regulations. "You may know *of* God by looking at the rules and doctrines, but you will never intimately know God."

To *know someone*, in the original language of the Bible, is to have *intimate and personal knowledge* of that person. You may know *of* many people, but with how many do you have intimate and personal knowledge? This is how Adam (Genesis 4:1) *knew* his wife Eve. He knew her intimately, and therefore conceived children.

True salvation is more than simply forgiveness of your sins; it is a relationship of intimacy. God wants your obedience, yet He also desires and hungers for your love and your friendship. This reconciliation and intimacy is made possible through the finished work of the cross, and not through your own works, your sacrifices, or even your good deeds. When you truly surrender your heart to God, then God will also have your good deeds and your service. Your heart will be led by the spirit of God, and will begin to lead your flesh to align with your spirit. But simply doing good deeds and sacrificing will never produce a relationship or intimate fellowship with God.

***

"So how do you pray, then, Jenny? Don't you ever sin and then ask for forgiveness?" Snyder asked. "Do you ever sin in your daily walk?"

"Sure. The good news is that as a Christian, you are now dead to sin, and sin does not hold you as its slave."

Jenny was essentially telling Snyder that he should begin to focus on God, not the sin. I heard once of a minister of the Gospel, who, when asked if he still sins, replied, "I'm not too sure…I don't really pay attention to it." This man was God-conscious, not sin- conscious! "I choose to focus upon the finished work of the cross and my Savior, Jesus, not on the sin of this world!"

This man understood his place in Christ Jesus! As did Jenny.

"I can pray this way now, Snyder. It is all about God. You have to keep it all about Him. Let your prayers remind you of your place in Christ, the grace and mercy of the finished work of the cross. Note how it does not allow for the self-condemnation and guilt that can pull you down in your walk with Christ. *Thank You, Lord, for forgiving me of my sins. Thank You that Your grace and mercy allow me to walk into Your presence, as I am being transformed by the Holy Spirit. I am being transformed into Your image from glory to glory, as You are in me. Thank You, Lord. Amen!"*

Your Notes:

"Repent, for the kingdom of heaven is at hand,"
-John the Baptist

Chapter Eleven

Repent & Change Your Life For *Ever*

Repent, release, receive, remind, and rest. If you truly desire the transforming power of God in your life, if you really want transformation, take hold of the truth that will set you free! In the following chapters, we will examine these five "R's." Meditate on them, and ask God to help you work them out in your own life for a radical U-turn!

Repent

"Repent, for the kingdom of heaven is at hand," said John the Baptist. What is repentance? Is it simply being sorry for what you have done? Is it praying a sinner's prayer or joining a church? Or is there something more to repentance? Walking through the desert and proclaiming his message aloud, John's entire ministry and his entire life up until he started prophesying the message of Christ, was all based on one word… repent! What was this repentance he cried forth to a lost and dying world?

Jesus Christ Himself began His message the same way: "Repent, for the Kingdom of God is at hand." *Repent.* It's a simple word, a word that holds in itself the key to eternal life, and it's the first step in the transformational power you need to truly change.

We see the word numerous times throughout the Bible, in both the Old and New Testaments. Look closely at the two passages below:

> *"And it came to pass, when Pharaoh had let the people go, that God led them not through the way of the land of the Philistines, although that was near; for God said, Lest peradventure the people <u>repent</u> when they see war, and they return to Egypt:"* (Exodus 13:17 KJV).

> *"And Moses besought the Lord his God, and said, Lord, why doth thy wrath wax hot against thy people, which thou hast brought forth out of the land of Egypt with great power, and with a mighty hand? Wherefore should the Egyptians speak, and say, for mischief did he bring them out, to slay them in the mountains, and to consume them from the face of the earth? Turn from thy fierce wrath, and <u>repent</u> of this evil against thy people. Remember Abraham, Isaac, and Israel, thy servants, to whom thou swearest by thine own self, and saidst unto them, I will multiply your seed as the stars of heaven, and all this land that I have spoken of will I give unto your seed, and they shall inherit it for ever. And the Lord <u>repented</u> of the evil which he thought to do unto his people"* (Exodus 32:11-14 KJV).

The Lord repented...of what? Does this mean God made a mistake and asked Moses' forgiveness? Hardly. Moses was simply asking God to change His direction, to change His mind, and reconsider the destruction of the Israelites. The context of the word *repent,* that is, godly repentance, comes from the Greek word *metanoia,* which means to *change one's mind and purpose, to turn from our purpose and toward God's purposes.* Moses was asking God to move from one path to another.

For instance, when Snyder appealed to the judge with sorrow for breaking the law, sorrow over his destructive lifestyle, he had hoped the judge would have mercy on him and grant his freedom, that the judge would not exact punishment. However, freedom at that stage would not be justice. Justice must be dealt out to the guilty one who has broken the law. The purpose of God's law is the same: to show us that we are guilty, that punishment is inevitable to the lawbreaker, and as a means to help us change direction, which can be a process. Henry Ward Beecher, an American abolitionist and clergyman (1813-1887) said, "Repentance may begin instantly, but reformation often requires a sphere of years."

The Law Reveals

Paul tells us that the law is a schoolmaster, that he would not even have known sin were it not for the law that revealed it to him. Jenny tried to explain this to Snyder.

"Have you ever received a speeding ticket?"

"*Have* I, uh-huh!"

"How did you know you were guilty, that you deserved the ticket?"

"Well," said Snyder. "The sign on the side of the

road that showed the speed limit didn't jive with what my speedometer read."

The road sign clearly posted the law, and it was clear that Snyder had broken it. Now, did the speedometer condemn and judge Snyder for breaking the law? Of course not. Snyder knew he was guilty because he could use the measure of his speedometer against the clearly-marked speed limit. The Law of God is similar in that it is our signal, our guide and measure to show us that we have broken the law God has clearly placed before us. It also informs us that to break it, is to break the law, for which there are consequences, penalties to be paid.

Would a judge in court dismiss the traffic violation if Snyder appealed it with sorrow for committing it? Not if the judge was a just and righteous judge. Clearly, the law was broken; Snyder had to pay for his violation. You might argue, "Wouldn't a loving and kind judge forgive?" Sure, he might; but would that be just and fair? Jenny tried to explain this to Snyder, but finally had to open up and reveal a painful personal secret to help him understand. This horrifying piece of her life would be difficult to recount, but she felt she needed to share it with her friend to make her point.

Jenny's Confession

She was only seven when she witnessed a crime so horrific, it would haunt her, and forever shift her life. This crime was against her mother, by a beast who brutally raped her, as Jenny watched, helpless, from her bed. Clutching her pillow in terror, she cried out above the screams of her mother, and the vulgar voice of the attacker. But a sudden sickening blow to her mother's head silenced the dark room, and mommy's voice forever. Jenny trembled as she finished her story, and Snyder sat silent, not knowing what to say. Then she continued, telling Snyder of the jury who had found her mother's murderer guilty, of the judge who asked him, "Any last words before sentencing?" and of the rapist's sorrow for his crime. "I am sorry, I shouldn't have done it. I won't do it again."

"Snyder," said Jenny, "her murderer was truly repentant. It was a sincere apology. Given that, do you think this guy should have escaped punishment?"

He understood now. There was no way a righteous judge could let the guy off scot-free. Justice had to come to those who had suffered. Justice to Jenny, who had to watch her mother die a brutal death; who spent every birthday since without the one whom she adored; who would graduate and marry, motherless. Justice would have to come to her father, suddenly without his soul mate, and to the many friends left behind.

"The judge *had* to sentence him, didn't he, Jenny?"

Nodding yes, she dabbed her eyes with a lock of her hair. "The point I'm trying to make to you, Snyder," she said, "is that being sorry for one's sins is simply not enough. The penalty of sin is death – someone has to pay the penalty of our sins. God is a Righteous Judge who sentences the guilty and exacts penalty on every law ever broken, including our sins, no matter how sorrowful we are over our actions. But He loves us so much, that He sent

One to die for our sins. He sent a perfect sacrifice. Jesus Christ, who became sin. The only one who could pay it for us, was the Lord Jesus Christ. When you accept Jesus, you are accepting His perfect sacrifice as payment for all of your sins.

"We sin, Jesus pays the price. True repentance is not only about being sorrowful over our sin, but about changing our direction, turning from a life of sin and destruction, turning our lives over to God and to His will for our lives."

"Jenny, so what you're telling me is, because God is a righteous, just, and fair judge, He has had no choice but to exact a sentence of death for sin. Because He loved us so much, He sent us Jesus, His only Son, to pay the penalty for those who truly desire to change directions, turn from sin, surrender to His will."

"Exactly!" Jenny nodded her approval, and silently thanked God for bringing light out of a dark memory. This was turning into a healing time for her…who knew?

Liberation

Repentance is your first transformational step. It is liberating! Have you truly repented? Remember, repentance is a process, not a one-time sorrowful plea or a magical, instantaneous antidote to all of your problems. Rather, it is a conscious and willful turning- away-from; a changing of direction, toward God's perfect will for your life. True repentance is sincerely praying, "Thank You, Lord for Your sacrifice. I accept it, and I am turning my whole life over to You. Please change me, transform me, and forgive me. I want what You want for me, and I want to follow You."

Your Notes:

"Let Go and Let God"

Chapter Twelve

Release the Works!

"Let go and let God," Jenny told Snyder, concerning his burdened relationship with his fiancée, which was unraveling. Through his personal turmoil and challenges with addictions and still questionable lifestyle, and their burgeoning problems, he held on by a thread to the hope of salvaging the relationship.

"You are trying to do something in the flesh that God wants to do in the spirit," she continued. "You must turn this issue *over to* God; release it into His hands and allow Him to work."

"I've asked God for help! I have *begged* Him to help me. When will He do it?"

Jenny shrugged. "He may be doing it already, and you can't see it yet."

"But it hurts…"

"That's because you haven't really released it and turned the situation over to God. You are trying to fix things by yourself. Have you…have you released it to God, Snyder?"

Snyder was not sure that he had; hence his turmoil and frustration.

***

We actually limit, hinder, slow, and even stop the progress of God's hand and work in our lives when we attempt to go it alone, or do things our way in fixing our problems or even in transforming our own lives.

I vividly recall a powerful New Year's Eve church service that I attended during a time that I was lost in a lifestyle of sin. My heart had been focused on worldly desires, and I had come to an impasse. It was actually a pit of anguish, and I was teetering on the edge, even contemplating suicide as I soaked in my grief and despair. This particular night, I had hoped the pastor's sermon would speak to me, that God would send a personal message, "It's okay, I'm in control." But I couldn't focus on the sermon. It was like a blank canvas – nothing seemed to apply to me. The longer the preacher preached, the more uncomfortable I got, even seated in the comfortable padded pew. Nothing about my life was comfortable, though; and I was restless and yearning for answers and relief, something that no human being could give me. By and by, I almost willed the preacher to stop talking so that I could come up to the altar at the altar call, a place I knew I could call out for help. I marked my spot, set my eyes on the place up front where I would kneel, pray, and cry out to God. Finally, the pastor finished and invited people forward, and I was there in a flash.

"God says He is trying to do it, but you are in His way," whispered a woman as I knelt, already crying to God. I thought, *How could I ever be in God's way, as powerful as He is*? It didn't make sense. But God spoke again through the woman, giving her words of knowledge concerning my life. He brought revelation to me concerning how I had limited His mighty work in me by failing to fully release everything into His hands, for good! Here I had prayed, cried, and daily begged God to handle things, to give me peace and resolution concerning several challenges; yet as soon as He started His mighty work, I'd pluck it from His hands, and try to do it my way. I wasn't persuaded, convicted in my heart that He would be able to keep and resolve what I had committed to Him.

"...I am persuaded that he is able to keep what I have committed unto him until that day." (2 Timothy 1:12)

Surrender in Deed

"I surrender, Jesus...I surrender it all to You," I cried out that evening. It was more than lip service, actually surrendering in coming days, in my deeds. It was a process, to be sure, as I learned and sought to trust God and His faithfulness to handle situations, even though I might not have instantly seen a manifestation of a resolution or healing. I realized that whenever in the past I had tried to make things better myself, I had been interfering with what God was accomplishing in the spirit and through others concerning situations and people. This is what caused my impatience, my anguish, my depression, and my pain. This is what brought me to that do-or-die precipice where my only choice was to release it once and for all, to God.

What are you holding on to in your life? What situations in your life do you want to see changed, but are failing to fully release into the hand of God? God is faithful to keep what we commit unto Him. This is a monumental promise of God that we often overlook in the above-noted scripture. Meditate on it. Are you persuaded that He is able to radically turn things to the good in your life? God Almighty is faithful to keep what you have committed to Him, faithful with what you have handed to Him. This truth transformed my mind-set and my life, and it can transform you.

Have you truly committed aspects of your life to God, surrendering them in word *and* in deed? Embrace His promise.

***

Snyder was facing drug addiction, immoral sexual desires, and a world of confusion about the Christian walk. Surrendering and releasing his problems over to God's power and glory would be the only way that he could withstand the trials and temptations of life, the only way permanent change could come to his life. But he didn't quite know how to release his issues to God.

"It is something we learn to do, and must continue to do continuously," said Jenny. "It's a process."

"Kind of like the glory-to-glory process of transformation …right?"

"Bingo!"

Snyder got it, finally understanding that releasing and surrendering is a process that allows the Holy Spirit to work through us.

Release Means "Let Go!"

Releasing something to God is actually letting go and turning it over into God's hand. The problem we usually face is letting go only long enough to finish our prayer, only long enough to speak words of surrender and faith in His manifestation power. And then, before we even let God grasp His hand of provision over our problems, we snatch our problems back with a clutched fist of doubt and fear. When fear, doubt, and impatience overtake us, we do not allow God to move in His perfect way. We snatch the concerns out of His mighty hand and back into our own hands of fear.

We do release in words, by confessing our release, by confessing to God that we trust Him to keep what we commit to Him. We do this by praying to God and offering Him our *life*. When we begin to realize that God is in all things, and that He is concerned with every area of our life, our prayer life will change. Instead of begging and pleading, or even arguing with God, prayer time becomes a time of thankfulness and confession of our faith in *His* ability to handle our situations.

"Lord, I commit to You my life, my spirit, and my soul. I acknowledge You in all things, and I thank You for being my Lord. That is how I pray," Jenny shared. And she prayed it often, not to remind God (as if He needs to know), but to remind herself of the fact that it is not her problem or situation any more, but God's. And He can handle it!

When you begin a prayer life that includes

surrendering your situations over to God and confessing that He is your Source and Provider, powerful and unique things will happen!

First, your faith to overcome issues will greatly increase, as you realize that your issues are not yours alone. Your issues are now God's concerns.

Second, His mighty hand will work in divine ways you could never even imagine. As your faith increases, you open up to the miracle-working power of God. Faith and comfort manifest so that you can now "see," and have an awareness and confidence of the work being done on your behalf.

Assurance Is Yours!

Often I think back to working with my father whenever my car broke down, or I happened to wreck my car! I was very certain I could not repair the car in most cases, and probably could never afford to pay someone else to repair it. But I always had a peace and certainty within me, true faith that when I needed help, my father was there for me. "Daddy will fix it," I often spoke, with absolute confidence that he both could and would. My certainty almost became a joke with my friends and relatives, who would say, "I know, I know, Larry will fix it." He always did. We must learn to have such faith and assurance whenever we engage our Father in heaven in prayer! When you can release with your words, thoughts, and actions, your confidence and assurance in His divine intervention on your behalf, you will have truly released the issues over to the One who can handle it all, our Lord God.

Your Notes:

"Blessed be the God and Father of our Lord Jesus Christ, who has blessed us with every spiritual blessing in the heavenly places in Christ." (Ephesians 1:3 NKJV)

Chapter Thirteen

Become a Wide *Receiver*

"Ask and you shall receive..."
– Jesus Christ

Paul penned an incredible message to the church at Ephesus. *"Blessed be the God and Father of our Lord Jesus Christ, who has blessed us with every spiritual blessing in the heavenly places in Christ."* (Ephesians 1:3 NKJV)

We must learn how to slow down and truly delve into the meaning of God's words, because they are loaded with promises for His children. He promises to *bless you* with not one or two, or a few, but with *every spiritual blessing*! How profound is that? I wonder how many blessings there are: hundreds, thousands, unlimited?

***

"The fact is really simple," explained Jenny to Snyder over coffee one day. He had expressed concern over a particular challenge that he could not overcome. The two had grown close as friends; not only for the spiritual aspect, but Jenny talked Snyder's language, "football," and could keep up on the stats with any sports jock. He felt comfortable around her, and she was a walking example of godly transformation. She'd been through a lot, but wasn't a defeatist. He liked that about her; and he was growing spiritually, so he was all ears.

"The blood sacrifice of Jesus restored your place of blessings, your place of healing, and your place of life itself. However, Christians in particular are ignorant of the finished work of the cross. Oh, yes, we have little problem accepting John 3:16, the love of God that offers salvation to the world. But we skimp, skim, or squirm over His other promises, finding them harder to grasp, or even accept as related to us personally. Jesus paid the price for your sins, yes, Snyder; but He accomplished so much more for you, for all of us. His blood sacrifice redeemed us from a life of curses and damnation! His blood sacrifice released *all* spiritual blessings to believers."

"We kind of shortchange ourselves, don't we?" said Snyder, watching and laughing as Jenny dumped a mountain of sugar into her coffee. She wasn't shortchanging herself on the sweet stuff. He left his black, as if to teasingly stress his self-control in the absence of hers -- although he had to fight off the temptation to add a shake of cinnamon and a dollop of whipped cream to his own cup.

"Uh-huh," nodded Jenny. "Listen, pal, if you are not living a life of victory or you are still under the power of a satanic stronghold, then the problem is not with God, but with you."

She was on to his antics. "Hey, pass the cream, will you?"

He passed the stainless steel container to her, but she ignored it, and then switched the subject back to football and the plays of the previous night's game.

"Will you give me the cream, Snyder?" she said

sipping her coffee. Snyder pointed to the pitcher and rolled his eyes. "It's right there, in front of your nose." *Good grief, what was wrong with this girl?*

She continued drinking the steaming coffee without pouring any cream into it. *What gives?* thought Snyder. He always teased her that she might as well be drinking a milkshake, the way she dolled up her coffees.

Jenny reamed off some Super Bowl stats, and once again, asked for the cream. But this time, she asked more politely. *"Please* pass it to me." Again he pointed to it. *What was wrong with her? There it was, accessible, but she was blind to it, and drinking her coffee anyhow.*

Suddenly she came unglued. "PLEASE GIVE ME THE CREAMER. NOW! I REALLY WANT THE CREAMER! PLEASE!"

She had what she desired, yet she continued to beg for it.

Enough was enough. Sternly, Snyder chided. "Jenny, you already have it. Why are you still asking me? I can't give you again what I have already given you!"

Her face relaxed, and she grinned. "I asked you repeatedly to drive home a point, and you took the pigskin for the touchdown. I knew that creamer was there, but what I demonstrated was a problem in receiving it. Your problem is not in your giving things to the Lord, but in your receiving things from Him."

***

This scenario may seem ridiculous to you, but this type of begging and praying for what we already have bombards the throne room of heaven every single day! "Lord, please bless me…heal me…prosper me…save me…" and God responds, "I already have." But we continue to ask, even though our blessings, our healings, our prosperity, our salvation is in front of us. We settle for living without it, even though it has been given to us already. As Jenny emphasized to Snyder, and as Paul emphasized to the church, we have already been blessed with all spiritual blessings. Thus, the problem never lies with God, but rather with the receiver him or herself, the one praying.

This is not to condemn you or riddle you with guilt, but to shed light on this subject so that you can experience transformation and success in your prayer life. The Bible reminds us that the lack of knowledge causes people to perish. This is the knowledge we lack: that we already have our answers in the promises that have been provided. They are just waiting for us to receive them!

Got Yer Ears Up?

As a child, I remember having to "tune in" our television channels by adjusting the rabbit-ears antenna atop our television set, or by my uncle adjusting the antenna on our roof. Eventually, we would get a clear picture. The television signals, although invisible to us, were available to us if we were willing to tune in to a station's frequency. No amount of begging, pleading, or even crying out could change a frequency or signal that was already out there waiting to be received. Calling the television station was fruitless: the problem wasn't their signal, but our receiver.

You have been *(past tense-already done)* blessed, the Word tells us. By His stripes you were *(past tense-already done)* healed. All your needs have already been provided for! His blood sacrifice is sufficient for all your needs, and anything that was provided by the Atonement is already yours. Simply receive.

***

"I need help with my drug addiction. Shouldn't I pray for help?" Snyder asked.

"Yep. However, once you pray for the help and healing that He has already provided for you, you need to receive it into your life. Remember how I would have had to pick up the container and pour out the blessing of abundant cream for my coffee?"

"But how do I receive it…healing from my addictions, for instance?"

"By faith," Jenny replied. "You take God's word as *truth,* and show your faith and belief in His promises by your words and your actions. You take a stand of faith, and you step forward in expectation of God's word as truth."

Full of Faith, yet Unbelieving

You will always go through this process. Your ability to receive will depend on your faith, and on how you handle the inevitable unbelief. Reading of the Word of God, and filling your spirit with the Living Word, is nourishment that develops faith. Unbelief, however, is also always at work against the believer. What is commonly misunderstood is the fact that it is very possible to have both faith and unbelief working simultaneously in your life.

Let me illustrate this for you. After my son was born, we often ran a little late for Sunday morning church service, although we tried hard to get there on time. One Sunday, we were particularly late, and people were already in our favorite pew toward the back of the church, so we took a remaining empty one, right up front by the altar and preacher's podium. It became clear why the Lord had supernaturally intervened and placed us there. Everything was going great, when suddenly, the preacher's grown son stood up, in extreme pain. He had been battling kidney stones and had taken a turn for the worse.

"Let's pray, *now*," said the preacher's wife. We joined in prayer, as did the congregation, and the Lord spoke, through interpretation, for the church. "If you believe, I will perform a miracle here today. If you do not believe, then leave My house! I cannot perform a miracle where there is unbelief!"

All we needed was mustard-seed faith, but faith nevertheless. If it could move mountains, it could surely remove a painful kidney stone. God was revealing a poisoning and deadly mixture of unbelief in the atmosphere that would hinder a manifestation of healing.

In the Scriptures, we see that the disciples could not heal the boy afflicted by a demon. Jesus explained to them that unbelief prevented the boy's freedom from demonic bondage. We do see that Jesus delivers the child, as the child's father admits to Christ, "I believe... and help my unbelief."

We are all tempted to doubt at times. However, we know it is *unbelief*

- when we doubt all the time,
- when we focus on what won't happen, or what is not happening,
- when doubt becomes a fostering thought, much more than a fleeting one.

Ignorance, Disbelief, Sin-fixation

There are three main components to acts of unbelief. The first stronghold in this realm is ***ignorance***, which is a lack of knowledge in a particular situation. A person may be very knowledgeable in mathematics, for example, yet like a deer caught in the headlights when it comes to science, history, or art. The same applies to the Word of God and His promises that apply to our situations. This lack of knowledge causes our despairing moments. And you've heard me quote Hosea 4:6 before, God's people perish for lack of knowledge. The antidote for unbelief caused by ignorance is actually knowledge! Equipping yourself with the knowledge of God's Word will renew your mind with truth, and, as we are reminded in John 8:32, the truth shall set you free.

Another stronghold in the realm of unbelief is *disbelief.* Disbelief actually arises from misinformed teaching. God's Word is all too often taught in error, sometimes out of ignorance and oftentimes from doctrines derived from the desires of self-interests. One of the biggest problems in discerning the Word is in not grasping the differences between the Old Covenant and the New Covenant, under which we now live. The attempt to live a life under Old Covenant beliefs and doctrines while we are actually under the New Covenant is only going to cause us discomfort and pain. We continually strive for a standard that we can never reach, and that we are no longer called to strive for.

Another issue with misinformed teaching is the performance-based mentality on which a previous chapter shed light. When people believe they are good enough, they also believe God will bless and prosper them. Too often, we believe God *can* do whatever we need, but that He just chooses not to bless us because we are not quite good enough.

"When I am more like God, I will be blessed more."

"Jesus will heal me when I pray more often."

"When I give more to the church, God will bless me more."

Sometimes it is not a lack of faith that we have, but an abundance of unbelief born of religious lies! Our faith in God can be great, yet unbelief can cripple us!

Finally, our natural senses surge unbelief to the surface as we focus our eyes upon a world decaying in sin and hopelessness. We look death and sickness in the eye through our loved ones who are fighting or who have lost the battle; or those pulled under by a current of addictions; or torn asunder by poverty, or lack. We see immorality, sin, and disease -- yet we cry out for forgiveness, provision, health, peace, joy. Although we may believe in God and in His mighty hand of provision, sometimes allow unbelief access, and it trickles into our lives.

Seek and Ye Shall Find!

There is another type of unbelief, caused by holding back from receiving what has already been provided. The answer here is seeking and knocking on the door of truth. "Seek and ye shall find. Knock and the door will be opened." When you seek, you shall find, and the truth will come alive in your spirit!

If God's people perish for lack of knowledge, is that not even more reason why we should make a conscious effort to absorb knowledge, to overcome and to be victorious? Of course it is! This is why the apostle Paul told Timothy to study to show himself approved. Reading and absorbing the Word will bring life to the seed of faith within us. It will likewise bring death to the unbelief that threatens to consume us as a choking weed would a productive garden.

Taking time to study what others teach us is crucially important, to assure that we are receiving truth. The Biblical record in Acts 17:11 tells us of a church in Berea where Paul preached. The church gladly accepted the Word, and they studied the Scriptures to see if Paul was speaking truth. Searching the Word is of utmost importance in this age of numerous false doctrines and false prophets or preachers. Note that Jenny always encouraged Snyder to seek the truth of what she said for himself. This would help him to discern, tuning up his spiritual senses to recognize the truth, and to quickly dispel the lies of the devil.

Our religious influence, whether it is several months or several decades old, seems to mold our beliefs permanently, and therefore our prejudices. Studies have shown that a vast majority of people, upwards of eighty percent in many cases, stay in adulthood within the same denominational group where they were raised in childhood. This tendency to stay within a certain group or belief system as taught in childhood also can carry over to new Christians, when they relate back to their first religious encounters or teachings. The tendency toward exclusivity, however, is slowly beginning to decrease as our culture becomes more diverse, and a wider availability of information stretches throughout denominational borders.

Our current information age makes information readily accessible. We can research and study the Scriptures much more easily than just a decade ago. A quick Internet search will bring up dozens of Bible translations, commentaries, and literally thousands of contrasting interpretations from a vast myriad of beliefs. In addition, as we are more mobile and our network of influential friends and colleagues grows, our own set of beliefs and prejudices is always being challenged and stretched in our journey towards the truth. Fading away are the days of exclusivity within the church body of believers. There was a time when a Baptist would marry a Baptist, and then raise their children in... you guessed it... a Baptist church. Then there was a time when a Methodist would marry a Methodist, and raise their children in... a Methodist church. Today we see people from one denomination marrying people from another denomination, or a non-denominational church altogether. "Our way" of doing church is being replaced with God's way, as our differences gently force us to finally seek *God's* truth and *God's* divine way. Amen!

Seek the truth, and you will know the truth. Jesus Christ is The Truth, and as we allow Him to transform our hearts, we will see truth manifest in all of our ways. When we have The Truth manifesting truth within us, the enemy has no room there to foster unbelief.

Your Notes:

"We are all too often consumed with our focus on the sin and our prejudices towards the sinners. Damning people before we can even reach them. Damning ourselves as we look into the mirror of our own lives, before we can let the Holy Spirit complete His transformational metamorphosis within us."

– Wayne Sutton

Chapter Fourteen

Remind Yourself: GOD IS GOOD

Snyder had one hidden thought that kept creeping back up to the front of his mind. Regardless of his prayer time, nor how many times he heard Jenny declare to him that he was righteous, the thought continued to surface with paralyzing fear and condemnation.

"Why do I keep sinning?" Snyder felt ashamed and confused. Even though he tried to live a holy and righteous life, he still sinned -- daily. Not less sin, either…sometimes it seemed to be even more sin than before.

Sin has a surefire way of stepping into the limelight, doesn't it? The secular world already does a good job of it, glamorizing it or embellishing it into something palatable, displaying it on marquees as good for us. But we, as individual believers, tend to spotlight sin in our own lives, as well. We linger too long on it, despairing over it when we should be re-adjusting our focus. Are you lingering on your sin so that it consumes your thoughts and imaginations? If so, that focus will rule and bear down on you. A tightrope walker always keeps his or her eyes on one target and one target alone: the other end of the rope. Not down, not up, but only at that final destination. Not to stay focused on the right place is a potential death sentence. Where are *your* eyes?

Scripture reminds us that the eyes are the lampposts to the body. It even says that if the eyes are full of darkness, then the whole body will be full of darkness. It follows, then, that if the eyes are full of light, then the whole body is full of light. Set your eyes on your addiction, and you'll be a druggie forever. Set your eyes on your lack, and you'll always be poor.

What Consumes You?

The writer penned this truth by the unction of the Holy Spirit, to direct and lead our eyes as we survey the broken world in which we live. In many cases, the church body has reverted to a life focused on the sins of those around them. We focus on the sins of the world, and with laser-like focus, aim in on the sins of those inside the church. We see sin every day. We hear sin everyday. We imagine the sin of the world everyday. And soon enough, we live out the sinful deeds ourselves. Why all the focus upon our sins and shortcomings? This misdirected church focus is yet another deception from the pits of hell.

As Christians, we are usually quick to point out what we consider an act of sin. We are therefore very quick to identify those we consider sinners. We gossip about the sin or sinners, we spread rumors about the sin or the sinners, we preach against the sin and sinners, and sometimes we even have enough heart and compassion to actually pray about the sin and the sinner. Our focus, however, always goes back to the sin or the sinner, instead of to God our Savior!

Sin happens. Sinners are real. There is a solution, however; and as Christians, we hold the solution to a lost and dying world. We hold the very Savior within us, and

He is crying out to us, "Let Me out!" The Holy Spirit cries to believers, "Let Me out! Reach your world with My love."

Instead we are too consumed with our focus on the sin and our prejudices towards the sinners. Damning people before we can even reach them. Damning ourselves as we look into the mirror of our own lives before we can let the Holy Spirit complete His transformational metamorphosis within us.

When we maintain or linger our focus upon sin, we actually are allowing it to darken our entire body. We allow sin to overtake and control our thoughts, and even our actions. We give power to the sin when we keep our attention on it. The Holy Spirit will transform us into His image as we behold Christ, not sin! "What you focus upon will consume you…whether good or evil makes no difference."

If we want to experience change as a Body of believers, if we want to experience change in our individual lives, we have to do as God tells us to do in His Word.

Light dispels darkness. The light in our eyes fills our body and dispels the darkness. The light in the eyes of the Church dispels the darkness in the Body of the Church. It is time we focused not upon the sickness, but on Jesus the Healer. It is time we focused not on the lack, but on Jesus the Provider. Remember Him! It is time we stopped focusing on our sin: instead, we need to focus on the Forgiver of Sin. It is time we stop focusing on the shortcomings of others: we need to direct our focus on the Savior who pulls at their hearts, calls them to surrender to His sweet yoke of salvation. We need to see God working, praise God for His workings, and shed light on His workings, to the glory of God!

See Christ, not the sin. See Christ – see revival! See Christ – see transformation! Bold statements, yes; but my urgings are from the unction of a bold Holy Spirit within me. Stop praising the devil and his already defeated plans, stop giving him credence. This lowers our faith and hinders a move of God. Ignore the pathetic devil and his schemes, which are inconsequential and hold no power against you. Where we train our physical and spiritual eyes will determine our destination, and the destination of the Church! Far too many people have been hurt beyond reason within its walls just because of a misdirected, misaligned focus. We have to get hell out of our churches! We have to speak, act, bring in the Light, and dispel the darkness that damns and condemns.

> *"Finally, brethren, whatever things are true, whatever things are honest, whatever things are just, whatever things are pure, whatever things are lovely, whatever things are of good report; if there is any virtue and if there is anything praiseworthy, meditate on these things". (Philippians 4:8 NKJV)*

The Apostle Paul tells us to think upon the positive and good things in our life. He held a revelation of which we all need to catch a glimpse. When our thoughts are upon that which is good, we will see good manifest in our lives and those around us. When we see and think upon the good, we are acknowledging and honoring God. Likewise, when we see and think upon the evil, then we are only acknowledging and honoring Satan and his diabolical and cunning works. Remind yourself of Christ's words: *"It is finished!"*

Think upon the good things! These are not idle words; they are, rather, sage advice. It is virtually impossible to keep your eyes upon sinful deeds and entertain positive thoughts. You can never have your eyes set only upon sickness and think healing. You can never see a sinner as just a sinner, and expect to see God move in his or her life. You must learn to see what is good in a person's life. If you cannot see any good, learn to see God tugging at his or her heart; see that possibility through your God-given eye of faith; see the person as a child of God.

"Let there be light." - God

As a born-again Christian, you are righteous and blameless before God Almighty. Now. Today. You are made holy; and God not only loves you, but He also accepts you as you are, even in your old flesh. Remind yourself of that, moment by moment. God doesn't need reminding of that fact – but you do. It behooves you, if you don't want to sink in the world's quicksand, to remind yourself of the goodness of the Lord, and of how He thinks of you, in spite of what the enemy hurls at you to the contrary.

The world is quick to judge – but even quicker to judge the believer. Renew your mind-set: live, act, and breathe as one who is loved, adored, and accepted by God just as you are. Do this, and transformation will take hold!

Don't put up with Satan's lies. Speak the truth, shed light, and dispel the devil.

"You are not righteous..." whispers the enemy.

No! I have been transformed, sanctified, made holy and righteous!

"You are just a sinner..." chides the enemy.

No! I am a beloved, blood-bought child of God!

"You are always failing..." says the enemy.

No! I can do all things through Christ, who gives me all the strength I need!

"You will fail again..." predicts the enemy.

Get thee behind me, Satan! Jesus gives me life! He is my Strength. My Buckler. My very present hope in times of trouble!

"God is angry at you..." the enemy lies.

He will never leave me or forsake me; nothing can separate me from His love!

Remind the enemy of who God says you are!

Pour your heart into the promises of God! Pull them out, and employ them for effective results.

- You are God's child. -John 1:12

- As a disciple, you are a friend of Jesus Christ. - John 15:15

- You have been justified. - Romans 5:1

- You are united with the Lord, and you are one with Him in spirit. - 1 Corinthians 6:17

- You have been bought with a price and you belong to God. - 1 Corinthians 6:19-20

- You are a member of Christ's body. - 1 Corinthians 12:27

- I have been chosen by God and adopted as His child. - Ephesians 1:3-8

- You have been redeemed and forgiven of all your sins. - Colossians 1:13-14

- You are complete in Christ. - Colossians 2:9-10

- You have direct access to the throne of grace through Jesus Christ. - Hebrews 4:14-16

Are you starting to see the promises we have in our salvation with Christ Jesus? Remind yourself also of the following truths:

- You are free from condemnation. - Romans 8:1-2

- I am assured that God works for my good in all circumstances. -Romans 8:28

- I am free from any condemnation brought against me and I cannot be separated from the love of God. - Romans 8:31-39

- You have been established, anointed and sealed by God. - 2 Corinthians 1:21-22

- You are hidden with Christ in God. - Colossians 3:1-4

- You are a citizen of heaven. - Philippians 3:20

- You have not been given a spirit of fear but of power, love and a sound mind. - 2 Timothy 1:7

- You are born of God and the evil one cannot touch you. - 1 John 5:18

Find more truths in the Word of God. Bring to remembrance words of knowledge and prophecy over you. Write here, what you know to be true!

Your thoughts:

Remind yourself and remind the enemy that when Jesus said, *"It is finished,"* He was serious. It is finished, and you are now in the very hands of God Almighty, and that is worthy of praise! I leave you in this chapter with one last verse to meditate upon and let manifest deep into your spirit. Remind yourself of the promise we find in Philippians 1:6 – *"I am confident that God will complete the good work He started in me."*

Your Notes:

"Come to me and I will give you rest..."

– Jesus Christ

Chapter Fifteen

Rest in Jesus

"Come to me and I will give you rest..." – Jesus Christ

The book of Jude, verse 24, tells us that Christ will both keep and preserve us. With that one promise this chapter could both start and end; yet we will examine it further, so that you can secure revelation of what wonderful promises of restful bliss we have in Christ Jesus.

> *"Now to him who is able to keep you from stumbling, and to present you faultless before the presence of His glory with exceeding joy" (Jude 24 NKJV).*

Resisting, struggling, suffering, attempting, failing, and searching... Snyder found himself in the same condition as many others have, and do, as he walked the path of Christianity: exhausted. Exhaustion is even worse for those who are still lost, however; they are struggling and trying in vain, in a life doomed to despair and neglect. Yet their map and compass does not even include a savior. Their life is consumed with the false assumption that they can do it alone -- believing they need only to try harder, push themselves a little further, search for the truth in this broken world.

Exhaustion has only one cure, one resting place, and it is Jesus Christ. Jesus, the One who promised us rest when we come to Him. Jesus is the One, the only One, the

One and Only, the One whose promises are always true and always a secure foundation for your life.

"Come to me and I will give you rest..." Jesus promises. Snyder read this promise to himself on countless occasions as he faced struggles and trials. Nevertheless, his daily walk remained lined with despair, the choking yokes of bondage and heavy burdens ever prevalent.

If Jesus promises Snyder, you, and me this type of rest, then why does the exhaustion seem to overtake us at times? To answer the question, we must look back a few chapters and revisit the fact that we *have* (past tense) been blessed with all spiritual blessings, as promised in Ephesians 1:3. We also have been given the rest and peace of Christ for this life. The problem does not lie in the grantor of that promise, but instead lies within us who receive the promise… us.

We must learn how to receive and experience rest in Jesus. Spiritual rest is of utmost importance for our victory over strongholds, our transformation, and the realization and fruition of our divine destiny. We are aware of the antidotes to physical and emotional exhaustion. A nap, a vacation, a massage, a good book, counseling… it doesn't take rocket science to figure it out. But we are often oblivious to the need for spiritual rest, which is the antidote to spiritual exhaustion, and which comes by way of Jesus. We need relief from the deepest issues that plague our lives in respect to walking out our Christian life, to running the race, and finishing well.

***

How in Hell Can I Change? 157

"I'm so tired of trying," confided Snyder. "Up, down, this way, that way, pull, push, forward step, back step, leaps over tall mountains, falls into deep valleys… it is all I can do to remain upright." This was Jenny's opportunity to help her friend hunt down and deal with the little foxes that so consumed his spiritual energy and resolve.

"Check this out," said Jenny, pointing to Matthew 11:28-30. "Read it for yourself, out loud!"

"Come unto me, all you who labor and are heavy laden, and I will give you rest," it says, said Snyder.

"Go on," urged Jenny, "read more."

"Take My yoke upon you and learn from Me, for I am lowly and gentle in heart, and you will find rest for your souls."

"How about that?" interrupted Jenny. "Jesus will give you rest, and you will find rest for your soul! That, my friend, is an awesome two-thousand-year-old promise, but it still stands! Now for the finale: go for it!"

"For My yoke is easy and My burden is light…"

"Amen! Don't you see, Snyder? Jesus gave us the antidote to our frustrations. It is as simple as ABC, and D!"

<u>A</u>bout Face: *Come to Him*

This is the first test of obedience. Are you

trying to handle your issues with your own understanding, or are you coming to Jesus? Jesus not only desires us to come to Him with our burdens, but also commands us to do so. No problem is too filthy, too disgusting, too minor, too gigantic, for Him. Nor is any person too bad for Him. Even a rapist or a vile pedophile can come to Him and He will help, for He said, *"Come to me <u>all</u>..."* The "all," are those who seek true rest, according to His instructions. This invitation is for those who desire more than knowledge, more than church, more than salvation. It is for those who desire to embrace and behold Christ Himself, those who desire intimacy and connection with Him. The desire for *relationship* with Him is requisite to finding rest in Him, rest for your spirit.

<u>B</u>ring It to Him: *Surrender your labor and burdens*

Rest comes to those who resolve to quit laboring, to stop trying to overcome or accomplish something by one's own strength or efforts. Self-effort is trying to balance the scales between good and evil in order to appease God. When we surrender to Christ our self-efforts and our sinful deeds, we can rest, no longer having to carry the weight of the sin nor the fatigue from our unavailing efforts. To be heavy-laden is to be over-burdened; and, as we have learned, carrying the excessive weight of sin (such as focusing too much on it) is one way in which we over-burden ourselves.

Too many people carry the weight of shame and guilt along with them during their daily walk. This heavy burden prevents them from experiencing the full joy and peace that comes from relationship with God, from having the courage or even the wherewithal to move forward to achieve the life that was destined for them. In the completed work of the cross, you can lay down the guilt, unshackle the chains of condemnation, and lay aside the shame of sin and despair. In the completed work of the cross, you can fully rejoice in the arms bearing true and fully sufficient rest.

Cloak Yourself with the Yoke: *Take it!*

"My yoke is easy." Many people are familiar with Jesus' assurance, but few understand what a yoke is, and why Jesus referred to it. A yoke is a device that joins a pair of draft animals. It usually comprises a crosspiece with two bow-shaped pieces, each enclosing the head of an animal. The yoke enables the two to walk as one, and so is indicative of a helper in one's daily walk and load of life. It is no longer just you: it is you "in yoke" with Jesus Christ Himself! Within the promise of an easy yoke as part of this union between man and Christ, is the promised rest!

Snyder often placed his neck straight into man's yoke, which, if you study Acts 15:7-11, is a yoke of rules and a religious system of striving to earn God's acceptance. Though this is a popular way of trying to relate with our Heavenly Father, this yoke is *not* one you want around your neck! Snyder found rest by accepting the yoke God offered to him. Notice, it is a choice. Moreover, the consequences of not choosing His yoke are struggle, strain, and pain. Our choices do matter.

The yoke also symbolizes two people walking and

working together, no longer one person with one direction, but instead two people headed in one direction. Two examples might be Jenny and Snyder as friends working out their faith, or a man and woman brought together as one in the covenant of marriage as husband and wife. A wife cannot be yoked to a spouse and walk her own way, and vice versa. The yoke affects the outcome for the other. If one member yanks and pulls, bucks or rears, the other will get hurt. Each has to walk in unity with the other. Likewise, we cannot be yoked to Jesus, and walk our own way. But we can be assured of a smooth journey, because He is lowly and gentle in heart. Our yoking with Him thus affects our eternal life, because it leads us heavenward. Being yoked with Jesus means that we won't be confused; we will know which way to turn, what is safe or not, and truth or not. God is not the author of confusion. You know who, *is*.

Determine the Truth: *Learn From Him*

"Learn from me..." – Jesus Christ

Once we have come to Jesus and accepted His grace, we have a responsibility to actually *learn* from Jesus, as He Himself noted! How true. The Holy Spirit revealed this to me at a summer youth camp where I volunteered. *"I will teach you many lessons,"* He said, as I prayed and worshiped Him in the spirit after a commissioning service. How it startled me to hear His voice so clearly! I didn't know whether to fall prostrate on the floor, or jump to the rooftop to praise Him. But had I wanted to do either, I couldn't have; I was glued to my chair, and all I could say, stammer really, was, "Teach me, Holy Spirit, oh, teach me!"

If you ever wanted to be a teacher's pet, here is your chance! There is no better teacher than the very Spirit of God! Become His devoted student! His divine lesson plans will open the very windows of your soul to peace.

Yearn to Learn

Learning to learn from Him was a process. But the more my soul yearned for rest in Him, the more wisdom and knowledge I desired from Him as His student. And learning didn't always look the same. Sometimes you just want to bask at His feet, seeking a quiet place to listen. He may teach you through a sermon or from the words to a hymn or song, or via a word of knowledge given to someone concerning you. Or, of course, revelation or inspiration is often found in the Scriptures. Perhaps His lesson for you will come with a dream, a vision, an angel, or something you read in a book. Some might hear His audible voice, or the still sweet voice deep within the spirit man. His voice speaks to many in nature. Perhaps a circumstance may occur in which He intervenes; His intervention will be a lesson eternally remembered. Life experiences, good or bad, can bring about needed direction or change. Many have fought tragic battles, only to look back and see that God's hand was always there, guiding and directing with a divine hand of love. Truth can be spoken to those who seek it, in a plethora of ways. Trust that the Holy Spirit can use any method He chooses to teach you! It is our responsibility to keep ourselves open to His lessons, and to learn.

***

Snyder was concerned that he hadn't learned well, or learned enough. He just couldn't seem to achieve a breakthrough. "I go through the same issues, over and over again. Why? Why do I keep repeating stuff?"

"Anything can be causing it," answered Jenny. "It could be a rebellious spirit, a double-minded mind-set, your own destructive lifestyle and poor decisions. Or consider this: perhaps God is trying to teach you something you haven't grasped yet!"

Snyder wanted more specifics. "Jenny! How would I know?"

"Try asking God, and seeing if what you are doing lines up with the Word. Are you within His will? Do you tend to blame God or others for your predicaments? Are you creating problems for yourself? Are you neglecting becoming an avid and eager learner?"

Great question to ask of Snyder. Sometimes we are slow learners and have to repeat a grade or two before we grasp or learn something God is trying to teach us. Some people fight the same battle repeatedly, though it may look different each time. Thankfully, God is patient, and the Holy Spirit will stick with us to teach and guide us in the magnificent process, from glory to glory.

I hope I have conveyed to you how vital it is that you accept the fact that God wants to teach you! Moreover, it's critical that you spend time in the process of learning, so that you can experience what you crave -- rest and peace in God! With proper rest, healing will manifest, and "revive all" will happen! Yes, divine rest carries revival to your body, to your life, to the church body, and to the world! With rest, you can reflect upon and appreciate the transformational changes, finally take a deep breath, heave a great sigh, and even crack a smile heavenward to the Father, acknowledging the love and grace He has given you. Rest in the Lord and in the finished work of the cross, and remember Christ's words: *"It is finished!"*

Your Notes:

"For I am convinced that neither death, nor life, nor angels, nor principalities, nor things present, nor things to come, nor powers, nor height, nor depth, nor any other created thing, will be able to separate us from the love of God, which is in Christ Jesus our Lord"

(Romans 8:38, 39 NKJV)

Chapter Sixteen

A Lifetime of Life Changing

The last time Snyder saw Jenny was during a Tuesday evening Bible study with friends. Neither knew it would be fourteen years before they would see each other again. Life sometimes has a way of taking us from one place to another rather abruptly. Preferably, we move in unity with Jesus, yoked with Him, trusting His lead. That lead may keep us at home, or send us to the ends of the earth, to the aid of a friend, or to a misdirected brother or sister in Christ. In Jenny's case, He led her to a new job in another town.

Snyder would miss the special friend he had found in Jenny. She was also a precious spiritual mentor and sister in Christ, who had taught him much, but not without sacrifice. It was necessary for Jenny to bring her own painful memories to the surface, so that he could learn and hope for his transformation. He felt confident, even in her absence, that he could break through, because her knowledge and victories empowered and encouraged him to experience every promised blessing, too.

Jenny knew Snyder would be okay. She couldn't grow him in Christ: that was something he had to learn from the Lord Himself, and choose to do. Never could she have imagined the awesome transformation God did create in him, once self-condemnation fled in light of the discovery of the truth.

Almost fifteen years had passed. Both of their lives and circumstances had substantially changed. Jenny hardly recognized him when her daughter introduced Snyder as her new Sunday school teacher.

"Pleased to meet you," Jenny said, without looking up, still smiling at her daughter, who seemed ecstatic with her new classroom teacher. "My name is…"

"Jenny," said the teacher, completing the introduction.

"Snyder?"

"One and the same."

For a moment neither could say a word. Both were overcome with emotion, colorful flashbacks, and a sense of celebration deep within their inner beings. This was more than a reunion of friends; it was a reunion of two searching souls who had found the unconditional love of God -- two souls, born of the same Spirit, reunited in the fellowship of Christian love.

"It has been a long time," said Snyder finally.

"I'll say… very long," agreed Jenny, trying not to appear too mesmerized by Snyder's metamorphosis. "It's not that you've changed physically: well, you have, I see a few wrinkles, a touch of grey… but that is not all I'm seeing. Your smile -- there is something different about it. You're at peace, aren't you?"

Snyder nodded tearfully. The Spirit of Truth had

done a great work in him.

Jenny's daughter broke the thoughtful silence. "Mommy, look at my picture. I colored the Ark of Moses!"

"You mean, 'Noah,' dear," Jenny said gently.

Snyder laughed. "Trust me, *that* she made up all by herself."

Suddenly it really hit home to Jenny. Who'd have thought it? Snyder was teaching her daughter about the love of Jesus, encouraging her every Sunday. What a turnaround, what a miracle! And she was certain her daughter would grow mightily in the Lord while in his care.

The reality is, God had a plan for Jenny and for Snyder, and of course, for Jenny's daughter, as He has for His beloved children, no matter their condition. God predestined a portion of Jenny's life toward guiding and directing Snyder at a time when the enemy was having a heyday playing with his mind. God used her because she was willing to be used by Him, and because she yielded her will over to God's will, allowing God to work through her. Snyder needed her guidance, her teaching, and her insights. He needed her fellowship to hold him up as he struggled with just how far he had strayed from God, and to lead him toward the Holy Spirit, who would renew and transform him.

Snyder found God more than once through his friend. How often in your life have you been where Snyder was, searching for hope and mercy while peeking through the veils of religion and the sins of the world? Perhaps you are currently called to live where Jenny was living, as a vessel through which God can work to reach a lost sinner, or to help build up and edify another. *Until* God. *Until* Jenny. *Until* that moment of truth. May God help us by sending a Jenny to us when we have our Snyder moments in life, and may God bless and equip us when we are needed to be an *until* person to someone else.

In Conclusion

By now, you will have found the answer to the title question of this book, "How in hell can I change?"

In summary, in case you have missed it, we will find change when we accept the fact that God desires relationship more than rules, obedience more than sacrifice, and love instead of damnation. Behold Christ in your heart, and rebuke the lies that advance from the pits of hell. You are truly loved by the Creator of the Universe, and He has you on His mind! Even now, as you are reading this conclusion, Christ's mind is set upon you. His heart is open for your love. Become a wide receiver, and receive that love, and the work of the cross, as your guarantee of victory.

> *For I am persuaded that neither death nor life, nor angels nor principalities nor powers, nor things present nor things to come, nor height nor depth, nor any other created thing, shall be able to separate us from the love of God, which is in Christ Jesus our Lord. (Romans 8:38, 39 NKJV)*

I invite you to slow down and let Christ work in your life, remembering that in His hands it is a divine process and *never* a crisis. Always ignore the lies that you aren't good enough, or don't measure up, whether you hear them in the church or elsewhere.

You can change if you desire change; but you won't change yourself. Christ will change you in a wonderful process called "glory to glory," a transformation that works from the inside, out. My prayers are with you and with everyone who is seeking change in their life. I pray that you can look across the valleys of despair and frustration, and expect to receive what has already been provided for by the ultimate sacrifice of our Lord Jesus Christ! Receive God's blessings for you!

I leave you with this additional hope and promise.

> *"Now the Lord is the Spirit, and where the Spirit of the Lord is, there is liberty. But we all, with unveiled face, beholding as in a mirror the glory of the Lord, are being transformed into the same image from glory to glory, just as by the Spirit of the Lord." (2 Corinthians 3:17-18, NASB)*

Sinner's Prayer

How YOU Can Receive Jesus Christ and Be Transformed by the Holy Spirit!

We are all born into sin, and all have fallen short of his glory. If you are not sure that your name is written in the Lamb's Book of Life (Revelation 21:27) then I plead with you to call out upon the name of the Lord Jesus. Pray the following prayer and receive him as Lord of your life.

Heavenly Father,

I know and acknowledge that I am a sinner. I repent, right now, of all my sins, and I am asking you to forgive me. You said in your Word, *"Whosoever shall call upon the name of the Lord shall be saved"* (Romans 10:13). And so, I am calling on the name of your Son, Jesus, to come into my heart and be my Savior.

You also said, *". . . if you confess with your mouth, 'Jesus is Lord,' and believe in your heart that God raised him from the dead, you will be saved"* (Romans 10:9). I believe with my heart that Jesus died for my sins and was raised from the dead so that I may have eternal life. I confess Him, right now, as my Lord.

In the name of Jesus I pray.

Amen.

*Now that you have prayed the prayer of salvation, know that you have made the best decision one can make. I encourage you to seek out a Christ-centered, Bible-believing church to cultivate your newfound faith – and remember that the spirit of God will transform you from Glory to Glory.

Need more encouragement? E-mail me today at: Wayne@TheSecondAdam.com.

Your Notes:

About The Author

Wayne Sutton is a minister, teacher, author, and seeker of truth from Wilmington, NC. His heart for writing was inspired by a love of teaching the truths of Jesus Christ to all who are willing to hear.

Although raised in a rather traditional Pentecostal background, Wayne searches for the true Kingdom of God, and the King Jesus, regardless of denominational beliefs and limiting boundaries. Wayne often reminds people that "God is bigger than your religion," as he ministers to people in all walks of faith and belief systems.

Wayne lives in Wilmington with his wife Candace and his son Kelton. Wayne is available for speaking engagements, conferences, interviews, or simply to bring the word and power of God to those seeking truth and a closer walk with God.

You can learn more about Wayne and his ministry online at www.TheSecondAdam.com or www.HowInHellCanIChange.com – you can also contact Wayne personally by e-mail at Wayne@TheSecondAdam.com

SPECIAL OFFER!

You are entitled to a FREE subscription to Wayne Sutton's newest online newsletter and podcast at our website **www.TheSecondAdam.com**

This informative newsletter and podcast, *"Straight Talk with Wayne Sutton,"* now reaches thousands of believers from numerous countries all over the globe; bringing teaching, prophetic revelations, and even detailed "how-to" step-by-step training in the ministry of the Kingdom of God.

Simply go to the website and sign up for your FREE online newsletters, podcasts, and FREE online books – and be sure to tell others about this FREE valuable resource. You can sign up now at www.TheSecondAdam.com. Do it today for a special FREE Gift!

To Order Additional Copies of This Book:

You can order online at www.TheSecondAdam.com or at the site www.HowInHellCanIChange.com with the options below:

Or you can send payment (including p/h) to:

TheSecondAdam.com Ministries
712 Southern Charm Drive
Wilmington NC 28412
(866) 869-9090

ORDER OPTIONS:

A. Individual Books – only $14.95 each plus $4.95 s/h per order – plus it will be autographed by Pastor Wayne, and a special prayer will be spoken over each and every book you order!

B. Our "Books of Hope" Program – only $14.95 per book! There are countless numbers of people who want our book, yet may not be able to afford even the small costs of $14.95 at this time. You can be a ray of hope in their lives simply by donating this important book to those in need. We have ministries here in the US and overseas that need this book.

When you order under our "Books of Hope" program, you receive one copy of the book, and then you simply choose how many people you want to help. You can receive the additional books at your address to give away as you feel led – or we will mail the additional books to ministries in need, as well as give them away to local Narcotics Anonymous and Alcoholics Anonymous groups here on the East Coast. *Each book we give away here locally will also be given away with a New King James Version Bible! And – inside of each book and Bible, we will <u>emboss it with your name as the donor</u>, and a note letting them know you are praying for them.

C. Small Groups – We have a special for small group settings. When you order 10 or more books (at a discounted rate of only $99.95 plus s/h), you will receive a special Leader's Guide (not available for purchase otherwise) that Pastor Wayne wrote especially for small group settings. This Leader's Guide will be e-mailed to you in PDF format so you can print it out and have multiple copies for every one participating! If you are involved in any small group sessions – <u>this is a must-have for your group</u>!

D. Churches and Conferences – If you are a Pastor or events planner – look closely! If you order 100 or more books (discounted rate), then Pastor Wayne Sutton will personally fly to your church or conference and minister the principles within the book to your congregation **<u>And Wayne will fly out to your event at his own expense</u>** within the 48 continental states! See the minister behind the book, as his heart pours out what God has shared with him – the power of the Holy Spirit to touch and change lives!

**Pastor Wayne has a limited schedule, so as you are considering – order now, and Pastor Wayne will personally call you and schedule his visit and details.*

Made in the USA